UNDERSTANDING BUS...

ECONOMICS
MADE EASY

Rob Dransfield
and
Donald Dransfield

Published in 2002 by
Nelson Thornes Ltd
Delta Place
27 Bath Road
Cheltenham
GL53 7TH
United Kingdom

02 03 04 05 06/10 9 8 7 6 5 4 3 2 1

A catalogue record for this book is available from The British Library.

ISBN 0 7487 6671 5

Illustrations by Steve Dallinger, cartoons by Nathan Betts
Page make-up by Paul Manning

Printed and bound in Great Britain by Scotprint

*The authors would like to thank Jane Gilby, Sandy Marshall and Paul Manning for their help in the
preparation of this book.*

Picture credits
Page 23: Milton Friedman Foundation (photo by Steven N. S. Cheung); 33: Corel (NT); 32, 48 and 49, courtesy of
the National Portrait Gallery, London; 52: Microsoft; 67: Hiroya Ito (http://www.beckham.tv); 92: courtesy of Trinity
College, Cambridge (photo: Kris Snibbe/Harvard News Office); 94, courtesy of European Central Bank.

Every effort has been made to trace or contact all copyright holders. The publishers would be pleased to rectify any
omissions or errors brought to their notice at the earliest opportunity.

Contents

Preface

Doctor Proctor – your friendly guide to the world of economics

This book has been written to help you develop a good basic understanding of economics, particularly as it applies to firms and the business world. As well as explaining some of the main analytical tools used by economists, it introduces key figures in the development of economic thought over the last two centuries and covers many of the major issues in economics today.

Economists are widely divided in their views about how the economy should be run. These differences result from their very different ideas about what economics is *for*. For some, it is a vehicle for providing more efficient markets. Others believe it should be concerned with wider social issues such as fairness in the distribution of incomes and other rewards.

The book begins by looking at some key economic concepts and tools. It goes on to examine a number of key economic issues that affect us all, and which are the focus of government policy-making, including employment, inflation, and sustainable development. It then looks at the key differences between the public and private sectors. After outlining the markets for factors of production and the economics of the firm, it ends with a survey of some of the important new ideas which are shaping economics today.

Doctor Proctor's aim is to make your study of economics lively and enjoyable. We hope that you find him a helpful and sympathetic guide.

About the authors

Rob Dransfield is a Senior Lecturer in Business and Economics at Nottingham Trent University, specialising in Environmental and Development Economics. He has also worked as an External Examiner at the University of Mauritius, MIE.

Donald Dransfield is studying economics at Trinity College, Cambridge. He has a particular interest in politics and macroeconomics.

How to Use this Book

As you work through the text, you'll find the following features to help you.

Key Ideas

These are some of the fundamental ideas on which economics is based.

You Must Know This

Terms and principles that you need to learn by heart and understand

Distinguish Between...

Here you need to be able to explain the difference between one term or concept and another.

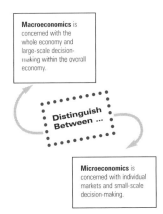

Doctor Proctor Calculates

Learn these methods of calculation – you'll save yourself a lot of time!

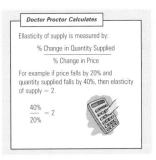

Doctor Proctor Outlines ...

Explanations of important themes and ideas in economics

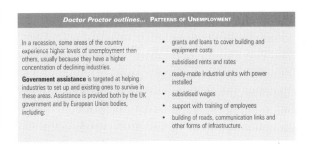

Questions and Answers

Short, practical exercises to test your understanding

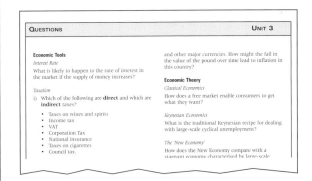

UNIT 1

INTRODUCTION

This unit shows why it is important to study economics. It also introduces a number of important ideas and concepts which are needed in order to understand the nature of economic decision-making.

Topics covered in this unit

1.1 The Importance of Economics
Understanding the economic forces that shape our lives. Scarcity and choice. The local, national and global economy. What is meant by 'economic decision-making'?

1.2 Economic Incentives
How economic incentives influence decision-making

1.3 Opportunity Cost
Economic choice and the sacrifice of the next-best alternative.

1.4 The Macro and Micro Economy
Understanding the difference between large- and small-scale economic decision-making

1.5 Supply and Demand
How supply and demand drive the market economy. The relationship between price and the quantity of goods demanded and supplied.

1.6 The Price System
The system that determines decision-making in most societies today.

Questions

1.1 THE IMPORTANCE OF ECONOMICS

Key Ideas 🔑

Scarcity and Choice

Why Study Economics?

Everyone should know something about economics because economic decisions affect us all. The more knowledgeable we are about economics, the better we can control the forces that shape our lives.

Using Resources

Economic decisions need to be made because we cannot have everything that we want: the earth's resources are limited relative to our needs.

For example, it is not possible to build a car park on a piece of woodland *and* use the land as a nature reserve. The same piece of metal cannot be used to build a chair *and* a desk. Choices have to be made. We can have *either* the car park *or* the nature reserve, *either* the chair *or* the desk – but not both.

The National, Local and Global Economy

The **economy** is the arena in which these decisions are made.

We use the term **national economy** to describe the geographical area in which decisions are made about national resources.

We refer to the **local economy** to describe decision-making in our locality, and the **global economy** to describe the economic system of the world as a whole.

Because the earth and its resources are finite, difficult economic choices often have to be made

Doctor Proctor outlines... ECONOMIC DECISIONS

It is important to distinguish between the main types of decisions that are made in an economic system:

- **what to produce** – e.g. military weapons or food?
- **how to produce** – e.g. high- or low-tech, mass production or small-scale manufacturing?
- **for whom to produce** – e.g. will the goods produced be shared by everyone, or will the best and most expensive goods go to those with the highest incomes?

1.2 ECONOMIC INCENTIVES

Key Ideas 🔑

Incentives

Individual economic decisions are influenced by **incentives**.

For example, the manufacturers of a soap powder may seek to persuade more customers to buy their product by claiming that their powder 'washes whiter'. The incentive here is the whiteness of the wash.

The government may seek to persuade motorists to switch to cleaner forms of fuel by taxing fuels which cause the most pollution. Here, the incentive is the lower tax (and the potential benefit to the environment).

Incentives offered by advertising or by government policy can have an important effect on consumer behaviour

---

Doctor Proctor outlines... INCENTIVE SYSTEMS

Different societies offer different types of incentives to economic decision-makers. There are two major types of incentive systems:

1 Until the late 1980s, large parts of Eastern Europe, China, Cuba and other countries operated centrally planned economies in which the government made most of the choices about how resources were used. This system was known as **state socialism**. The incentive here was the desire for equality and the 'greatest good of the greatest number'. Unfortunately, growth in living standards was slow, and hardship provided little incentive for people to pull together.

2 **Incentives based on price**. Today most countries use incentives based on prices as rewards. In a price-based economy, people work harder if they are paid more for their effort. In the same way, manufacturers produce more goods for the market if the price is high enough to allow them to make a profit. Under the price system people are essentially working for themselves. Their incentive is the opportunity to increase their own income through the price they are paid for their economic activity.

In practice, most societies combine elements of both approaches: a degree of government decision-making and central control, combined with decisions made through the price system.

1.3 OPPORTUNITY COST

Key Ideas 🔑

Opportunity Cost

Businesses need to consider **opportunity cost** all the time – the real cost of buying a machine may be that the business has to lay off workers. The opportunity cost of having an employee working on one project is the contribution he or she could have been making to another project at the time.

Dr Proctor says:
'You Must Know This!'

Opportunity cost is the sacrifice that is made when you choose one course of action and not another. It is the **sacrifice of the next-best alternative**.

Examples

The **opportunity cost** to the government of building a hospital may be a school – the next-best use of its money.

During the summer and autumn of 2000, 'fuel lobby' protestors demanded that the government reduce the tax on petrol. The prime minister, Tony Blair, argued that if the government lowered fuel tax it would have to reduce expenditure on items such as schools and hospitals.

In this case, the opportunity cost of cheaper petrol would have been a less efficient health and education service.

Money spent by the government on roads and transport inevitably reduces the amount available for hospitals and schools

1.4 THE MACRO AND MICRO ECONOMY

Key Ideas 🔑

Macro- and Microeconomics

A key distinction in economics is between **macroeconomics** – the study of large-scale or general economic factors such as interest rates and national productivity – and **microeconomics**, which looks at single factors and the effects of individual decisions.

Micro- and **macroeconomics** are closely related because they often use the same tools of analysis, such as demand and supply. However, the focus of attention is different: macroeconomics is concerned with the 'big picture' rather than individual cases.

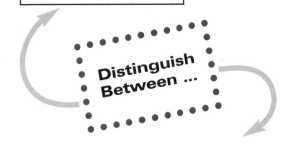

Macroeconomics is concerned with the whole economy and large-scale decision-making within the overall economy.

Distinguish Between ...

Microeconomics is concerned with individual markets and small-scale decision-making.

Examples

Macroeconomics would be concerned with average price increases for all goods and services in the economy. Microeconomics might focus on what determines the price of an individual good, e.g. the price of CDs.

Macroeconomics might be concerned with whether average incomes are rising for people in the economy as a whole, whereas microeconomics might be concerned with why the incomes of Premier Division footballers are higher than those of National League ice hockey players.

Trying to explain the causes and effects of unemployment in the UK as a whole involves macroeconomics. Studying why unemployment in Luton is rising would involve microeconomic analysis.

The micro and macro economy

1.5 SUPPLY AND DEMAND

Key Ideas 🔑

The Role of Price

Dr Proctor says:
'You Must Know This!'

The relationship between price and the quantity of goods demanded and supplied is governed by the laws of supply and demand.

In a **price-based economy** such as that of the UK, the price of a good or service acts as an important signal:

- For **consumers**, price is an important consideration in deciding whether to make a purchase. If the price is too high, consumers will be reluctant to buy.

- For **producers and sellers**, price will determine whether it is worth making or supplying a good or service. Rising prices will attract new suppliers into the market and encourage existing suppliers to provide larger quantities of goods. Falling prices will have the opposite effect.

Doctor Proctor outlines... DEMAND

The **demand** for a good is the quantity that purchasers are willing to buy at a particular price. The higher the price of an item, the less willing consumers will be to purchase it.

This can be illustrated by a **demand curve** showing the quantities of the item that consumers are prepared to buy at different prices. The following table shows the demand for CDs at different prices:

Price	Quantity Demanded
£5	4,000
£10	3,000
£15	2,000
£20	1,000

This information can also be illustrated in graph form, by plotting **Price** on the vertical axis and **Quantity Demanded** on the horizontal axis.

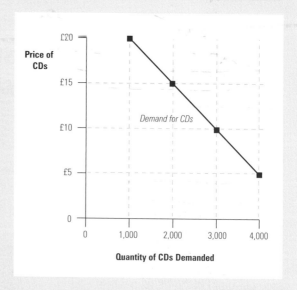

Note the typical shape of the demand curve, sloping down from left to right. This is because fewer people will be inclined to buy CDs if the price is too high.

1.5 SUPPLY AND DEMAND

Key Ideas

High and Low Price

Suppliers see prices in the opposite way to buyers.

- **Suppliers** find high prices attractive because a high price makes it easier to cover costs and to make a profit.

- **Buyers** are less likely to buy if the price is too high.

Doctor Proctor outlines... SUPPLY

As we have seen, rising prices attract new suppliers to enter the market and encourage existing suppliers to increase the quantity they supply.

The following table shows the supply of CDs at different prices:

Price	Quantity supplied
£5	1,000
£10	2,000
£15	3,000
£20	4,000

Again, this information can be illustrated in graph form. In the graph below **Price** is plotted on the vertical axis and **Quantity Supplied** on the horizontal axis.

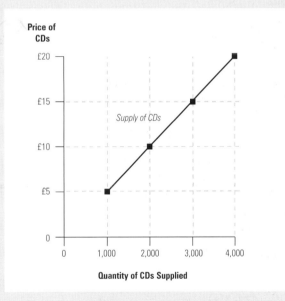

Note the typical shape of the supply curve, sloping up from left to right. This is because at higher prices the supplier finds it easier to cover costs and make a profit.

1.5 SUPPLY AND DEMAND

Key Ideas 🔑

Changes in Demand

Over time, demand for a good can change, so that more or less is demanded at the same price. There are many reasons for this:

1 **Tastes change**. For example, Michael Jackson was very popular during the 1970s and early 80s, and his CDs sold in huge quantities across the world. Today he is less popular. This means that a Michael Jackson CD will sell fewer copies at the market price today than ten years ago. The demand curve for Michael Jackson CDs can therefore be said to have **shifted to the left**.

2 **Changes in income.** A rise in incomes will lead to an increase in demand for many products. For example, some teenagers spend over £1,000 a year on CDs by their favourite artists. Given more spending money, the amount they would spend on CDs would increase still further. By contrast, a fall in incomes will lead to a reduction in spending on most goods.

3 **Changes in population**. A rise in population can lead to a **shift to the right** in the demand curve because there are more people buying goods than before. The **age profile** of the population is also an important factor influencing demand. For example, an increase in the teenage population will boost demand for Robbie Williams CDs. An increase in older members of the population is more likely to boost demand for classical music and CDs by the Beatles and Bob Dylan.

4 **Changes in the price of other goods**. The demand for goods is affected by the price of goods which are **complements** or **substitutes** (*see below*).

Price of Michael Jackson CDs

Old Demand Curve

New Demand Curve

Quantity Demanded

Doctor Proctor outlines... COMPLEMENTS AND SUBSTITUTES

The demand for goods is affected by the price of goods which are **complements** or **substitutes**.

- **Complements** are goods which are used together, such as a CD player and a CD. A fall in the price of CD players is likely to encourage the purchase of more CDs. A rise in the price of CD players will lead to a reduction in the number of CDs bought.

- **Substitutes** are goods which can be used instead of each other. For example, it could be argued that CDs and pop videos are substitutes for each other. A rise in the price of pop videos would encourage the purchase of CDs, and vice versa.

1.5 SUPPLY AND DEMAND

Key Ideas 🔑

Changes in Supply

In the previous section we looked at factors affecting changing demand. But **supply** can also change if economic conditions alter.

Farming is a good example of an industry where supply can change because of external conditions. With a good harvest, the supply curve will shift to the right, showing a higher quantity being supplied to the market at each and every price, compared to a poor harvest year.

Doctor Proctor outlines... FALLING COST AND THE SUPPLY CURVE

In recent years improvements in technology, particularly associated with the internet and computer software, have helped to reduce costs in many industries – for example, the mass production of CDs. With lower costs, firms are able to supply more goods at the same price than before. Hence improvements in technology push the supply curve to the right.

Rising costs push the supply curve to the left

Improvements in technology push the supply curve to the right

There are many reasons why costs might fall, varying from falling prices of raw materials and labour to reductions in government taxes, falling rents and lower interest rates.

Rising costs will lead to a shift in the supply curve to the left, as shown in the graph above.

Any changes in the cost of producing goods and services will cause a shift in the supply curve. A business faced with falling costs will be inclined to supply more because it is cheaper to do so.

1.6 THE PRICE SYSTEM

Key Ideas 🔑

Market Price

As we have seen, the **price system** plays a key role in determining what goods and services are produced, and in what quantities, as well as what goods are bought by consumers. But how does a producer know what is the right market price for his or her products?

Doctor Proctor outlines... EQUILIBRIUM POINT

When supply and demand are perfectly balanced, they are said to be at **equilibrium point**.

For example, the two diagrams below show the outline demand and supply curves for jars of strawberry jam in a particular week.

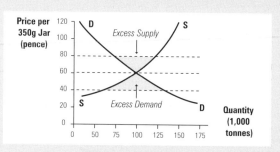

We can combine these two curves on a single drawing to illustrate how prices are determined in the marketplace. The point at which the two curves intersect is the point at which the wishes of both consumers and producers are met.

This is called the **equilibrium point** because there is nothing forcing a change from it.

- You can see that at a price of **60p** for a 350g jar, 100,000 tonnes of jam would be bought each week. At this price consumers are happy to buy 100,000 tonnes and sellers are happy to supply this quantity.

- At **80p** a jar consumers would be prepared to purchase only 75,000 tonnes and suppliers would be prepared to make 125,000 tonnes available to the market. At this price sellers would be left with unsold stocks and would quickly reduce supply to the equilibrium point.

- If the price were below the equilibrium – at, say, **40p** – demand would be for 135,000 tonnes with producers only willing to supply 55,000 tonnes; strawberry jam would be snapped up as soon as it was put on the shelves and stocks would run out. Prices would soon be raised towards the equilibrium point.

1.6 THE PRICE SYSTEM

Key Ideas 🔑

Market Price and Quantity Sold

In a market economy, changes in **market price** are the driving force that brings forward supplies of new goods and services.

Businesses are constantly on the lookout for fresh opportunities. When prices are on the rise, existing businesses and new businesses are attracted to move into the market by the prospect of higher returns on their capital.

Conversely, falling prices and declining markets are likely to deter potential new suppliers.

Examples

- Following the terrorist attack on the World Trade Center in New York in September 2001, worries about international security led to a fall in the demand for air travel. As a result, many airline companies cut back on supply, and several national carriers failed.

- In contrast, recent years have seen an increasing demand for leisure and fitness activities from consumers who are more aware of the benefits of healthy lifestyles. As a result, there has been a growth in the number of health and fitness clubs as more entrepreneurs have entered the market.

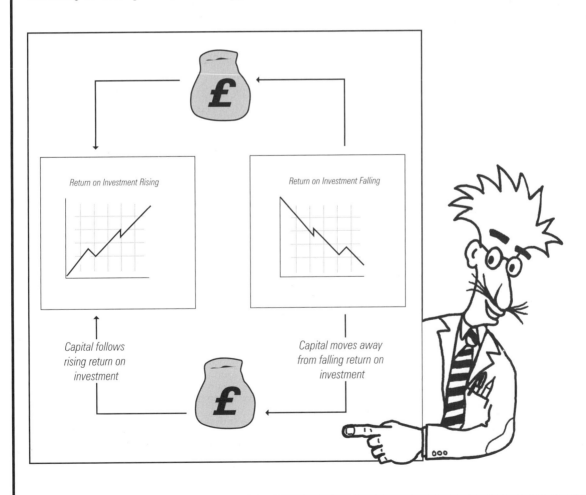

Return on Investment Rising

Return on Investment Falling

Capital follows rising return on investment

Capital moves away from falling return on investment

1.6 THE PRICE SYSTEM

Key Ideas

Elasticity

To describe the response in consumer demand to a change in price, economists use the term **elasticity**.

Producers or sellers need to know how much demand will change as a result of price changes so that they can calculate the effect on sales and on **revenue**, i.e. the amount of money they receive from sales.

- If demand for a product is **elastic** around the existing price, it may make sense to lower price in order to increase sales and revenues. It would be foolish to *raise* price, because sales and revenues will fall by a bigger percentage than the price rise.
- If demand for a product is **inelastic** around the existing price, it may make sense to raise price because revenues will increase. It would be foolish to *lower* the price, because even though a few more items would be sold, the gain would be offset by the overall loss of sales revenue.
- If demand is **unitary** for a product around the existing price, there is no justification for raising or lowering the price.

Doctor Proctor outlines... PRICE ELASTICITY OF DEMAND

Demand is said to be **elastic** if quantity changes by a higher percentage than price.

In other words, where elasticity measures:

- **more** than 1, it is **elastic**
- **less** than 1, it is **inelastic**
- **1**, it is said to be **unitary**.

Doctor Proctor Calculates

Elasticity of demand is measured by:

$$\frac{\text{\% Change in Quantity Demanded}}{\text{\% Change in Price (triggering change in demand)}}$$

For example, if the price of a good increases by 10% and this leads to a 20% fall in quantity demanded, elasticity would be:

$$\frac{20\%}{10\%} = 2$$

1.6 THE PRICE SYSTEM

Key Ideas 🔑

Price Elasticity of Supply

Elasticity of supply measures the responsiveness of supply to changes in price.

In the short term it is not always possible to increase the supply of a product. For example, if you have planted a crop in the ground, you cannot suddenly plant more simply because the price has gone up: the crop could take months to grow, by which time the price may have fallen again.

Doctor Proctor outlines... ELASTICITY OF SUPPLY

The term **elasticity of supply** describes how easy (or difficult) it is for a business to increase production of its goods or services. At a given moment, supply may be fixed. But over a few days, it may be possible to increase supply by using spare capacity or hiring more labour. In the longer term it may even be possible to build a new factory. Elasticity of supply can therefore vary over time. Generally speaking, the longer the time period, the easier it is to increase supply – i.e. make it more elastic.

The illustration below shows elasticity of supply in different time periods.

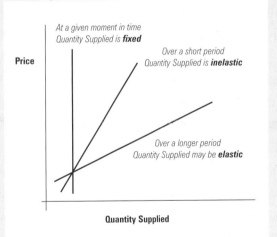

At a given moment in time
Quantity Supplied is **fixed**

Over a short period
Quantity Supplied is **inelastic**

Price

Over a longer period
Quantity Supplied may be **elastic**

Quantity Supplied

Doctor Proctor Calculates

Elasticity of supply is measured by:

$$\frac{\% \text{ Change in Quantity Supplied}}{\% \text{ Change in Price}}$$

For example if price falls by 20% and quantity supplied falls by 40%, then elasticity of supply = 2.

$$\frac{40\%}{20\%} = 2$$

The Importance of Economics

Classify the following according to whether they are decisions about:

a) what to produce
b) how to produce
c) for whom to produce

i)   The decision to increase government spending on education
ii) The decision by a company to introduce new technology
iii) A government decision to raise income tax on the rich
iv) A decision by a firm to concentrate on producing a few best lines and to cut out less efficient lines
v)   A decision by a firm to concentrate on producing goods for disabled people.

Economic Incentives

What sorts of incentive might be appropriate in the following circumstances:

i)   To reduce the amount of pollution produced by businesses
ii) To encourage people to work harder in a factory in the pre-Christmas period
iii) To encourage businesses to contribute more to community projects
iv) To encourage farmers to grow more organic produce

Opportunity Cost

John has been considering how to spend £20. After careful consideration he has ranked three alternative choices in the following order (with the preferred choice at the top and the least desirable at the bottom).

a) Spending the money on a visit to an ice hockey game, and spending the remainder of the money on sweets and drinks at the game
b) Buying a shirt
c) Travelling to, and watching, a pop concert.

What is the opportunity cost to John of making his preferred selection?

The Macro and Micro Economy

Which of the following are more concerned with macro- and which with microeconomics?

i) unemployment levels in the UK
ii) unemployment levels in Rochdale

iii) inflation in Europe
iv) the price of cheese in a local market
v)   the exchange rate of the Euro against the dollar
vi) the growth of living standards in a country.

Supply and Demand

In each of the situations below, explain what the likely effect on the demand curve will be for the newspaper, the *Daily News*.

i)   A rival newspaper, the *Daily Planet*, goes out of business.
ii) More people switch to newspaper reading and away from journals and magazines. This is because newspapers such as the *Daily News* begin to publish their own magazines and supplements.
iii) In a period of recession people cut back on general household expenditure.
iv) A newspaper with a similar format to the *Daily News* enters the market.
v)   The price of all newspapers increases.
vi) The average length of commuter journeys by train decreases.

In each of the situations below, explain what the likely effect on the supply curve for the *Daily News* will be:

i)   The cost of paper increases.
ii) New technologies make it possible to produce newspapers more quickly and cheaply.
iii) Average salaries of journalists increase.

The Price System

The following table sets out the demand and supply schedules for a particular make of sweet called 'Sweetsorts'.

Price of Packet (pence)	Demand (million packets per annum)	Supply (million packets per annum)
0	400	0
10	320	0
20	240	80
30	160	160
40	80	240
50	0	320
60	0	400
70	0	480

i) What is the equilibrium price? Why is this the equilibrium price? What volume of goods will be supplied to the market at the equilibrium price?
ii) Explain why 10 pence and 40 pence are *not* the equilibrium price.

Topics covered in this unit

2.1 Economic Growth
Ways of measuring
economic growth. The
importance of sustainable
growth.

2.2 Inflation
What is meant by inflation,
and how can it be
measured? The causes and
effects of inflation.

2.3 Unemployment
Methods of measuring
unemployment. The causes
and effects of
unemployment.

**2.4 The Balance of
Payments**
The importance of the
international trading sector.
How the balance of
payments account is
calculated.

**2.5 Other Economic
Goals**
The importance of equity
and sustainable
development.

Questions

Many economic decisions are made by individuals and organisations. But the government also plays an important role in making sure that the economy runs in an efficient and beneficial way. Often, difficult choices need to be made between conflicting goals and priorities. This unit looks at economic goals and the difficulty of achieving them.

2.1 Economic Growth

The idea of **economic growth** is that over time the total value of the economy (measured in terms of goods and services produced) should increase.

Is economic growth good for us? Until the last quarter of the twentieth century, most economists regarded economic growth as a 'good thing'. Today we are less sure.

Whatever the arguments, economists need to be able to measure economic growth in order to make comparisons with other countries and to compare past and present. Studying economic growth also helps to identify strengths and weaknesses in the country's overall economic performance.

Doctor Proctor outlines... National Income

Traditionally, economic growth has been measured using **national income statistics**. In the UK these are collected by government statisticians in what are known as the **Blue Books**.

There are three ways to calculate national income. Each should produce the same results.

1 Add together the total value of the **output** of industries, including only the new value created by each one. For example, if the car industry buys in inputs for £500 million and sells outputs of £600 million in a given year, it has created £100 million of new value in that year.

2 Add together the value of the **incomes** received by people in a country. This involves counting income from all sources, e.g. wages + interest + profits + rent.

3 Add together the value of **spending** in the economy. This involves counting up all **final expenditure**.

Example

To measure national income using the **final expenditure method**:

1 Add together all spending that converts into income for UK factors of production:

+ **C** Consumption Spending

+ **G** Government Consumption Spending

+ **I** Investment Spending (including Government Investment)

+ **X** Exports (goods and services sold by UK nationals to foreign countries)

+ **S** Subsidies to Businesses.

2 Deduct spending that does *not* convert into UK income:

− **M** Imports (goods and services bought by UK nationals from foreign countries)

− **Ti** Indirect Taxes (government taxes on spending).

2.1 ECONOMIC GROWTH

Key Ideas

Gross National Product (GNP)

Gross Domestic Product (GDP) is a measure of the income, output and expenditure produced by resources in the UK. However, UK citizens also own assets abroad, and foreigners own assets in the UK which generate income.

Property income from abroad therefore needs to be added to GDP and property income paid abroad needs to be deducted to give a figure for **Gross National Product (GNP)**.

Example

Step 1 shows GDP calculated by the final expenditure method *(see page 16).*

To calculate national income, we need to subtract net property income from abroad and make allowances for any depreciation in machinery and equipment in the UK in the year. This is shown in **Step 2**.

Gross National Product (GNP) is calculated by taking Gross Domestic Product and adding net property income from abroad. You would also need to add income from investments in foreign companies held by UK nationals.

Step 1

	£ million	
Consumer Expenditure	500,000	*Shows UK spending*
Government Consumption Expenditure	150,000	
Capital Formation (Investment)	100,000	
Total Domestic Expenditure	750,000	
Exports of goods and services	200,000	*Takes account of international trading*
Total Final Expenditure	950,000	
Less Imports of goods and services	225,000	
Gross Domestic Product at Market Prices	725,000	
Less Taxes on expenditure	100,000	*Takes account of the way taxes such as VAT and subsidies distort prices in shops*
Plus Subsidies	10,000	
GDP at Factor Cost	635,000	

Step 2

	£ million	
Gross Domestic Product at Factor Cost	635,000	*There is a net inflow of property income*
Net property income from abroad	5,000	
Gross National Product at Factor Costs	640,000	*Machinery and plant depreciate*
Less Capital Consumption	80,000	
National Income	560,000	

2.2 Inflation

Key Ideas

Controlling Inflation

A major objective of government is to control **inflation**.

Inflation is an increase in the general level of prices that is sustained over a period of time. General price increases may be slow (**creeping inflation**) or rapid, leading to **hyperinflation**.

It is important to keep inflation down because rising prices have the potential to destabilise the economy and, at worst, to lead to a loss of confidence in money *(see page 22)*.

The Retail Price Index

In the UK, inflation is measured using the **Retail Price Index (RPI)**. The RPI is based on records kept by 7,000 households which are surveyed across the country. This gives a picture of the 'typical items' bought by an 'average household'.

The RPI is usually known as the **headline rate** because it is frequently quoted in newspaper headlines.

Doctor Proctor outlines...
Calculating the Retail Price Index (RPI)

Each month, government officers record approximately 150,000 prices of some 650 different items up and down the country, as well as in different types of retail outlets. The average price of each of these items is calculated.

Each year new items are added to the Index to make it more representative of current spending patterns. For example, in 2002 leg-waxing entered the index and canned salmon was taken out.

Using this data the average inflation rate can be calculated. Each individual price change is given a 'weight', depending on how important it is in the typical household spending pattern. For example, food makes up about 15% of a typical household's spending, so a 10% rise in the price of food would raise average prices by about 15% of this – 1.5%.

The following table shows the weighting of different items in 2001 – but remember that these weightings frequently change.

Food	13.6%
Catering	4.9%
Alcohol	8%
Tobacco	3.4%
Housing	18.6%
Fuel and Light	4.1%
Household Goods	7.2%
Household Services	5.2%
Clothes	5.6%
Personal Goods	4.0%
Motoring	12.8%
Fares	2.0%
Leisure Goods and Services	10.6%

2.2 INFLATION

Key Ideas 🔑

Measuring Inflation over Time

In order to measure inflation, it is necessary to measure changes in prices over time.

The choice of a starting point or **base date** is very important. The aim is to choose a time that is 'normal' – i.e. when nothing abnormal or unusual is happening to prices. The base date is given an index of 100. We can then say, for example, that if in the year 2000 (the base year) the RPI stood at 100 and today it is 112, prices have risen by an average of 12%.

The following alternative methods can also be used to measure inflation:

1 **RPIX** (referred to as the **underlying rate**) excludes changes in mortgage interest. Mortgage rates are left out because housing costs account for a massive 18.6% of the RPI weightings and can distort the picture.

2 **PRIY**, or the **core inflation rate**, excludes changes in mortgage interest and in taxation. The Bank of England favours this measure of inflation.

3 **The Harmonised Index of Consumer Prices** is often used to compare inflation in the UK with other EU members.

Example

Suppose that households spend one-fifth of their income on housing, two-fifths on food, drink and tobacco, and two-fifths on other items. We can give these three categories weightings out of ten:

Housing	**2**	(two-tenths)
Food,drink,tobacco	**4**	(four-tenths)
Other	**4**	(four-tenths)

- In the year 2000 housing prices were on average £25,000 per unit, food, drink and tobacco prices were £1 per unit, and other prices were £3 per unit.

- In 2001 housing increased by 50% to £37,500 per unit. Food and drink rose 100% to £2 per unit, and other items stayed the same at £3 per unit.

These changes can be shown in a table as follows:

	Original index	New index	Spending weighting	New index x weight
Housing	100	150	2	300
Food, drink & tobacco	100	200	4	800
Other	100	100	4	400
Total				1,500

To find out the average increase in prices, use the following formula

$$\frac{\text{Total of New Index and Weights}}{\text{Total Weighting}}$$

i.e.

$$\frac{1,500}{10\,(2+4+4)} = 150$$

On average therefore prices have risen by 50%.

2.2 INFLATION

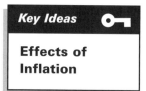

Not everybody suffers under inflation. Borrowers find that the amount they have to repay may be less than the amount they originally borrowed. Home-owners also may benefit because the value of their home may go up, while the real cost of the interest they pay on their mortgage may fall.

Inflation makes people unhappy. The effects of unemployment are probably worse, but, unlike unemployment misery, which affects only a minority of the population (even allowing for family members and those excluded from official jobless definitions), inflation misery affects *everyone*.

Doctor Proctor outlines... ECONOMIC EFFECTS OF INFLATION

Inflation gives rise to a range of economic and social problems:

Uncertainty – particularly in business. Firms that have sold goods on credit become more reluctant to do so, because they do not know how much the money they owe will be worth when the time comes for repayment. This makes life especially difficult for credit-based businesses.

A fall in purchasing power. As inflation increases, the value of money falls. Businesses find that they have to pay more for supplies and wages.

A fall in the value of savings. Savers find that their savings are reduced in value. This discourages them from saving, which makes it harder for businesses to borrow cheaply. The price of borrowing may increase.

Higher wage demands. Because the purchasing power of wages falls, workers demand higher wages. This pushes business costs up further, triggering an inflationary spiral.

Export problems. Rising prices in a country make it increasingly difficult to export goods because these goods are relatively more expensive than rival goods on international markets.

Time-wasting costs. As prices rise, businesses and consumers become less sure about prices and spend more time finding about the prices of goods when making purchasing decisions. This adds to costs.

Pricing administration costs. In a period of rising prices, sellers have to keep updating price lists and sales information. This in itself causes prices to rise.

Problems for those on fixed incomes. In a time of rising prices people on fixed incomes generally suffer. In particular, pensioners whose savings are not index-linked lose out as their savings fail to keep up with inflation.

2.2 INFLATION

Key Ideas

Theories of Inflation

Economists differ widely on the causes of inflation. Some believe that inflation is caused by too much demand – this is referred to as **demand-pull inflation**. Others believe that a major cause is rising costs – **cost-push inflation**.

In reality, inflation is probably the result of a combination of demand and supply causes.

Doctor Proctor outlines... INFLATION AND THE TRADE CYCLE

In Unit 1 we examined the demand for individual products, e.g. strawberry jam. This is sometimes referred to as **microeconomic demand**. **Macroeconomic** or **aggregate demand** consists of the general level of demand in the economy for goods and services. The demand for goods and services in the economy varies according to the **trade cycle**.

Over the past 165 years, the average rate of growth of real GDP in Britain has been 2% per year, which means that real GDP has doubled every 35 years. However changes in GDP have fluctuated with the business cycle. There are four distinct phases to a business cycle: **peak**, **contraction**, **trough** and **expansion**. Other frequently used terms for this are; **boom**, **recession**, **slump** and **recovery**.

A fall in real GDP (i.e. negative growth) over two successive quarters is referred to by economists as a **recession**. A very deep trough is known as a **depression**.

Milton Friedman, leading exponent of the monetarist school of economics

One group of economists described as the monetarists, led by the American Milton Friedman (*left*), believe that demand inflation is primarily caused by increases in the money supply. According to Friedman, 'Inflation is always and everywhere a monetary phenomenon'.

The monetarists' explanation can be summarised as 'too much money chasing too few goods'. Friedman argues that monetary inflation is usually caused by the government allowing too much money to be printed – often because it wants to spend more than it takes in taxes. Extra money pumped into the economy simply pushes up the price of goods.

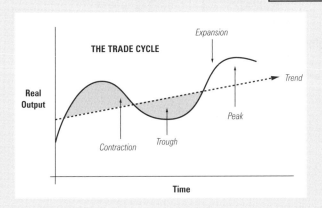

THE TRADE CYCLE

Real Output

Expansion

Trend

Peak

Contraction

Trough

Time

2.2 INFLATION

Key Ideas

Demand-Pull and Cost-Push Inflation

Cost-Push Inflation

Cost-push theories of inflation identify rising costs as the major cause of inflation. Rising costs can come from a number of sources:

1 **Rising import prices.** For example, in the 1970s spiralling oil prices added to inflation because fuel costs are a basic cost of production. A fall in the value of a country's currency can also lead to **imported inflation**.

2 **Rising costs of materials** in the domestic economy. For example, rising costs of basic agricultural products can affect prices in a range of food-processing industries.

3 **Rising costs of labour** resulting from higher wage claims – also increases in salaries paid to managers

4 **Increases in interest rates** add to the cost of borrowing for individuals and businesses.

5 **Rising taxes** can also push up costs.

Any of these **cost-push factors** are likely to lead to rising costs of production, forcing the supply curve for goods to shift to the left, so that the general level of prices rises.

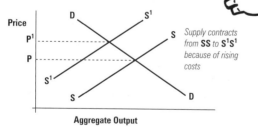

Supply contracts from **SS** to **S¹S¹** because of rising costs

Demand-Pull Inflation

When the economy is booming, it is possible that demand may outstrip supply, leading to **demand-pull** inflation.

The diagram below shows the relationship between aggregate (total) demand and aggregate supply in a boom period where there is full employment. (Note that aggregate supply is perfectly inelastic because all resources are fully employed so supply cannot be increased).

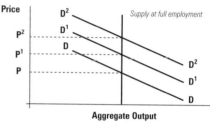

Demand increases from **DD** to **D¹D¹** to **D²D²**

Distinguish Between ...

2.3 UNEMPLOYMENT

Key Ideas 🔑

The Right to Work

A healthy economy is one in which **unemployment** is kept as low as possible, or preferably eliminated altogether.

The overall level of unemployment in the economy is closely related to the trade cycle.

In a downturn, large swathes of the labour force are laid off, and it becomes increasingly difficult to find work. The headlines on the right are typical of those on newspaper front pages at the end of 2001.

Widespread redundancies in air travel industry

Tour operators including Thomas Cook hard-hit

Fall in employment in tourism throughout the UK

The current Labour government believes that everyone has a right to work and that work is an essential form of participation in society. It regards unemployment as a form of **social exclusion**, since a person who is unable to work is prevented from playing a full role in society and from enjoying the benefits that society has to offer.

Doctor Proctor outlines... HOW UNEMPLOYMENT FIGURES ARE CALCULATED

Accurate unemployment figures are difficult to arrive at, and often it is in the interests of the government to make them look as low as possible. The figures often ignore part-time workers seeking full-time work and those on government training schemes.

There are currently two official methods of calculating unemployment in the UK:

1 **The Claimant Count** is based on the number of people claiming benefit and until 1997 was the main measure used for calculating unemployment. These figures were calculated by the Office of National Statistics. A major problem was that it was used only in the UK, and could not be used for making international comparisons.

2 **The Labour Force Survey**. Carried out by the **International Labour Office (ILO)**, this includes people without a job who are available to start work in the two weeks following their interview, and who have either looked for work in the previous four weeks or are waiting to start a job. These figures are taken from a survey of employment called the **Labour Force Survey** involving 6,000 households and over 100,000 adults. The survey gives a more detailed breakdown according to age, sex, ethnic origin, household size, etc.

The Labour Force Survey gives a higher figure for unemployment than the Claimant Count because it includes older, (often) male, workers who may be collecting a pension from a previous employer or being supported by their wife.

2.3 UNEMPLOYMENT

Effects of Unemployment

Unemployment can have a devastating impact on individuals, businesses, the community and the national economy.

The worst effects are:

- **Waste of resources.** Unemployed resources can quickly fall in value: machinery depreciates more quickly when it is not in use, and workers become less employable when they do not have the chance to update their skills. This reduces both the short-term and longer-term growth rate.

- **Demoralisation.** Unemployed workers become disenchanted with a society that cannot guarantee them a job. They become less inclined to retrain and will often feel less attached to their new employer when they eventually return to work.

- **Decline in expenditure.** Unemployment means that people have less money to spend. This further depresses the local and national economy.

- **Decline in investment.** As the economy moves into recession, fewer businesses make a profit, and there are fewer opportunities for investment.

- **Loss of government revenues.** As incomes decrease, government tax revenues fall. This means there is less money to spend on public services such as schools and hospitals.

- **Increases in government spending.** As unemployment figures rise, the government has to spend more money – e.g. in unemployment benefit – to pay for the services that the jobless cannot provide for themselves.

- **Social decline.** Factories, offices and workshops close down, leading to decay, pollution and environmental degradation. Demoralised communities are often characterised by vandalism and higher-than average crime rates.

Doctor Proctor outlines... PATTERNS OF UNEMPLOYMENT

In a recession, some areas of the country experience higher levels of unemployment than others, usually because they have a higher concentration of declining industries.

Government assistance is targeted at helping industries to set up and existing ones to survive in these areas. It is provided both by the UK government and by European Union bodies, and includes:

- grants and loans to cover building and equipment costs

- subsidised rents and rates

- provision of ready-made industrial units

- subsidised wages

- support with training of employees

- building of roads, communication links and other forms of infrastructure.

2.3 UNEMPLOYMENT

Key Ideas

Demand-Side and Supply-Side Unemployment

Distinguish Between ...

Supply-Side Unemployment

Supply-side theorists argue that unemployment is caused by weaknesses in supply, and that people are either being taxed too heavily, or that there is not enough competition in the economy. The solution is to make supply more efficient or to provide incentives (or at least, fewer disincentives) for people to supply more.

Suppliers can be encouraged by:

- lowering taxes

- eliminating barriers to competition

- stopping unfair trading practices by larger firms so that smaller firms are better able to compete.

As with inflation, there are two major theories of how unemployment is caused.

Demand-Side Unemployment

Demand-side theorists argue that there is not enough demand for full employment levels to be reached.

Causes include:

- consumers not spending enough

- business people not investing enough in capital equipment

- government not spending enough

- firms not exporting enough.

The cure is for the government to encourage more spending, e.g. by lowering taxes or raising its own expenditure.

2.3 UNEMPLOYMENT

Doctor Proctor outlines... CATEGORIES OF UNEMPLOYMENT

- **Cyclical unemployment** can be caused by downswings in the trade cycle, i.e. periods of recession. In a recession, spending, income, output and employment fall. This is mainly a demand-side explanation of unemployment.

- **Structural unemployment** arises from longer-term changes in the economy affecting specific industries, regions and occupations. For example, the demand for British coal has been in decline for many years, leading to widespread unemployment in areas such as the North Midlands, South Wales, Yorkshire, etc.

- **Technological unemployment** occurs when introduction of new technologies leads to job losses. For example, **Information and Communication Technology (ICT)** has wiped out many jobs in banking and insurance. However, it is important to remember that new technologies also create a demand for new types of employees – witness the dramatic growth of 'call centre' work in the UK.

- **Real wage unemployment** occurs when wages are higher than the wage necessary to create full employment. The **minimum wage** is sometimes cited as a possible cause of unemployment. Suppose, for example, that every member of the working population (20 million people) is able to get a job in the economy when the minimum wage is £4. If the minimum wage is raised to £5, then perhaps 5 million people may lose their job if employers are not willing or able to pay the higher price of labour.

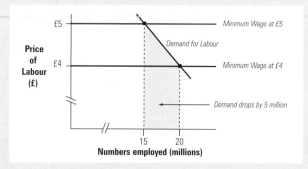

5. **Seasonal unemployment** involves workers being laid off at certain times of the year when demand for their labour is low. For example, in coastal resorts, unemployment is always much higher in the winter than in the holiday season.

6. **Frictional unemployment** occurs when people are between jobs or when they leave a job in order to look for other employment.

Unemployment is one of the worst social evils because it demoralises people. Some unemployment is short-term – for example, when holiday work ends at the end of the season. Other types – for example, unemployment caused by the run-down of a whole industry – are more serious and long-lasting.

2.4 THE BALANCE OF PAYMENTS

Key Ideas

International Trade

Key goals of international trading are to secure a high volume of exports and to avoid persistent **balance of payments deficits** (where the value of imports exceeds the value of exports).

International trade is important to any economy, particularly to an island economy such as the UK which has to rely on materials, goods and services imported from abroad.

For centuries the UK has gained enormously from international trade. We buy goods and services from other countries, and in return we sell goods and services overseas which are produced in the UK.

Dr Proctor says:
'You Must Know This!'

- An **import** involves the purchase of goods and services from overseas by a UK citizen, business or the government.

- An **export** involves the sale of goods and services overseas by a UK citizen, business or the government.

The volume of traded items
Volumes are measured in physical units, e.g. the export of 10 million tonnes of coal.

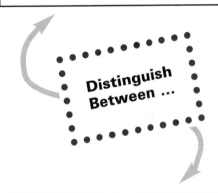

Distinguish Between ...

The value of traded items
Values of items are measured in money terms, e.g. £50 billion of exports.

Doctor Proctor outlines... VISIBLE AND INVISIBLE TRADE

All the tangible goods that we trade (i.e. things that we can touch and see) are called **visible items**. About 85% of Britain's visible trade is in manufactured and semi-manufactured goods, e.g. cars and electrical goods.

Services that cannot be seen or touched are called **invisibles**. About 25% of UK trade is in services, including financial services, transport, and travel.

2.4 THE BALANCE OF PAYMENTS

Key Ideas 🔑

Benefits of Specialisation

International trade allows countries to gain from **specialisation**.

The UK, for example, is able to concentrate on producing its most saleable goods and services, such as banking, insurance, whisky and bio-

technology. By trading these items on world markets we are able to buy goods which we would find it less easy to produce ourselves, such as pineapples, washing machines and Persian rugs.

Other reasons why we trade include:

• Some items, such as scarce minerals, are impossible to obtain in the UK
• To foster good relations with other countries
• To earn foreign currency
• Because we cannot fully supply our own market in many items.

UK exports are a vital source of foreign exchange. Since Britain joined the EU, the European market now accounts for over half of all UK trade.

Foreign trade allows UK firms to exchange home-produced goods with items which can be produced more economically abroad

Doctor Proctor outlines... THE UK AND WORLD TRADE

The UK is currently the fifth-largest trader in the world in terms of the value of imports and exports. Since Britain joined the EU, Europe has become our principal trading zone, accounting for over half of UK trade.

North America accounts for about 12%, and Japan and South East Asia are also important trading partners. Exports and imports to and from Eastern Europe are increasing in volume and value every year.

2.4 THE BALANCE OF PAYMENTS

Managing the Exchange Rate

An important task of government is to ensure a healthy balance of payments and to manage the **exchange rate**.

The exchange rate is the price of foreign currency in terms of domestic currency. If it falls, businesses will find that when they sell overseas, the value of what they receive in payment is less than before. If the exchange rate rises too quickly, it will be difficult for business to sell abroad because UK exports will be relatively more expensive than competing products from other countries.

Doctor Proctor outlines...
THE BALANCE OF PAYMENTS

The **Balance of Payments** is an account recording a country's international trade and its international borrowing and lending.

It has three elements:

1 The **current account** shows the value of imports and exports of goods and services. The UK frequently has a **deficit** on the current account. Often there is a deficit on visible trading, and, while there is a surplus on invisible trading, this is usually not enough to create a surplus on this part of the account. This is shown in the example below:

Visibles *(£m)*	Invisibles *(£m)*	Totals *(£m)*
Exports 200,000	Credits 200,000	Total Export Values 400,000
Imports 225,000	Debits 185,000	Total Import Values 410,000
Visible Balance − 25,000	Invisible Balance + 15,000	Current Balance − 10,000

2 The **capital account** records international borrowing and lending.

3 The **balance for official financing** shows the overall increase or decrease in a country's holding of foreign currency reserves. A deficit on the current account is adjusted on the capital account or by changes in the official reserves. The balance of payment always balances.

Balance of payments problems usually occur in the current account. These can arise when the current account is in deficit for a long period, leading to a drain on the country's reserves of gold and foreign currencies.

2.5 OTHER ECONOMIC GOALS

Key Ideas 🔑

Balancing Economic Goals

In order to achieve a **balance** between competing – and often equally desirable – economic goals, governments often have to make difficult choices.

For example, reducing unemployment can lead to an increase in inflation, and a reduction in the rate of economic growth can lead to rising unemployment. Often compromises have to be made.

As well as the key macroeconomic goals, there are other considerations which many people regard as just as important. Some of these are described below.

In the eighteenth century, the utilitiarian philosophers advocated the 'greatest happiness' approach to advancing the welfare of society.

Doctor Proctor outlines...
'THE GREATEST GOOD OF THE GREATEST NUMBER'

Jeremy Bentham (1748–1832) was the founding father of a school of thinking known as **utilitarianism**. To Bentham 'the happiness of society' was equivalent to 'the sum total of the happiness of all the individuals in society'.

Jeremy Bentham (1748–1832), founding father of utilitarian philosophy

Bentham argued that the guiding principle of right action is 'the greatest happiness principle'. Individuals should be allowed to pursue their own economic interests, provided this is compatible with the greatest happiness principle.

However, the problem is that, in seeking to maximise their own economic well-being, individuals may restrict the well-being of others.

In other words, in order for some people to be rich, others may have to be poor. If resources are scarce, it is impossible for all sections of society to enjoy them in equal abundance.

2.5 OTHER ECONOMIC GOALS

Key Ideas 🔑

Equity and Fairness

One of the most important economic goals for many people is that of **equity** or **fairness**. The problem with the concept of equity is that it is loaded with value judgements – what *I* think is fair might be quite different from what *you* think is fair.

For example, Margaret Thatcher stated: 'May all our children grow taller, but some grow taller than others'. What she meant was that inequality motivates people to be successful and improve their standard of living – and that this benefits society as a whole.

A different idea of equity was put forward by **Karl Marx (1818–1883)** – 'from each according to his ability, to each according to his need'. Here the emphasis is on everyone contributing as much as they can, and the rewards being distributed to those who need them most.

Karl Marx, co author (with Friedrich Engels) of the Communist Manifesto

Margaret Thatcher, Conservative prime minister of Great Britain, 1979–90

Doctor Proctor outlines... THE GOAL OF EQUITY

Equity is an important economic goal which is built into a range of government policies.

For example, the reason for taxing the rich at higher levels than the poor is to enable them to make a contribution to society which is proportionate to the benefits they have secured from society.
The current Labour Party philosophy of **inclusivity** is based on providing everyone with an opportunity to pay a full part in society.

In recent years the debate has focused on two particular aspects of equity: **intergenerational** and **intragenerational** equity:

Intragenerational equity is concerned with fairness to members of the *same* generation, i.e. all those living on the planet at a given time, rich and poor.

Intergenerational equity is concerned with fairness between one generation and the next. Being fair to the next generation involves handing on to our children *at least as much* as we inherited from our parents.

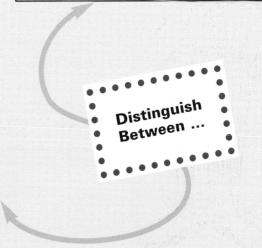

Distinguish Between ...

2.5 OTHER ECONOMIC GOALS

Key Ideas

Sustainable Development

An important goal of recent economic policy is to promote **sustainable development**. This means balancing economic, social and environmental objectives so as to maximise the well-being of people living now, without endangering the welfare of future generations.

The idea of sustainable development is in many ways a backlash against the tendency of economists to measure progress in terms of GDP rather than in terms of wider human and natural welfare indicators, such as life-expectancy, primary school attendance, access to clean water, freedom from disease, conservation of the environment, etc.

The growth model pursued in the West has brought remarkable benefits in wealth and in health, but it has also dangerously altered the balance of life on what Carl Sagan described as our 'pale blue dot'. Alleviating poverty is no excuse; nor is ignorance of the consequences really a convincing argument for a species that has walked on the moon, split the atom and mapped its own genome.

Doctor Proctor outlines... THE GOAL OF SUSTAINABILITY

Professor David Pearce in a series of books called *Blueprint for a Green Economy* has shown that if we are to move towards sustainability we need to consider four different types of capital that generate wealth:

- **Km** – Man-made capital, i.e. factories, machines, hospitals, etc.

- **Kn** – Natural capital, i.e. streams, rivers, lakes, forests, wildlife, etc.

- **Kh** – Human capital, i.e. the knowledge and skills of people acquired through education and training

- **Ks** – Social capital, i.e. family relationships and relationships within the community

Pearce argues that we have tended to focus on accumulating man-made capital at the expense of other forms such as nature and social relationships. We now need to act in a more informed way, taking account of the sacrifices that we make when we choose one action rather than another.

Four types of wealth-creating capital

Economic Growth

1 Name the three methods of calculating national income.
2 How can you convert a figure for GDP into national income, i.e. what do you need to add to and subtract from GDP to arrive at national income?
3 The table below compares GDP with total domestic demand. Why might domestic demand be higher than GDP in some months and years?

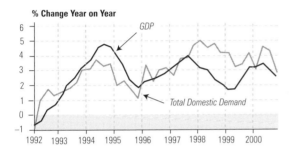

4 What is the difference between a 'cowboy economy' and a 'spaceship economy'? Which of these is a better reflection of the realities of modern-day living?

Inflation

1 What is the difference between the **RPI** and the **RPIX**? Why is the harmonised index of prices widely used today?
2 The chart below shows retail price inflation in recent times in the UK. Why might businesses welcome the pattern shown in the graph?

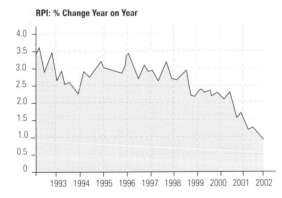

3 List three groups of people who are likely to lose out as a result of inflation, and two groups that are likely to benefit.
4 What is **imported inflation**?

Unemployment

1 How might the trade cycle be a cause of unemployment? Describe two other types of demand-related unemployment.
2 What measures can be taken to improve the supply side of the economy? Give three examples.
3 List three **negative** effects of unemployment for business.
4 The graph below illustrates a situation where the economy is at full employment with a wage level of £4.50. Illustrate the effect of imposing a minimum wage of £5.00.

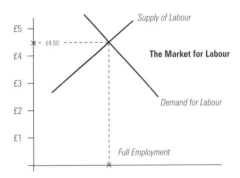

The Balance of Payments

1 Give three examples of visible exports *from* the UK and three examples of visible imports *to* the UK.
2 What is the difference between a **visible** and an **invisible**?
3 What are the **three** parts of the balance of payments account? Which part shows international borrowing and lending? Which part shows trading activity?
4 What is the **exchange rate**?

Other Economic Goals

1 Does **equity** mean the same to everyone?
2 What is **intergenerational equity** and how could this be achieved?
3 What is **intragenerational equity** and how could this be achieved?
4 What do you understand by the term **sustainable development**?
5 Does sustainable development mean that no form of capital can be reduced?

This data question about price changes is designed to pull together some of the learning from Units 1 and 2 of the book.

Inflation on the Run

Inflation indicates a general increase in the level of prices. In contrast the term **deflation** refers to a fall in prices. In recent times we have become used to very low levels of inflation – indeed, we are experiencing deflation in the goods market:

- Relative prices change in response to changes in supply and demand and advances in technology.
- Rises in supply tend to pull down prices.
- Falls in demand tend to pull down prices.
- Improvements in technology tend to pull down prices.

In recent years we have seen a massive increase in the production of goods on a global scale, supported by increased world trade. This has meant that the quantity of goods available, particularly in the USA and UK, has increased enormously.

In 2002 the average overall level of inflation in the **G7**, the group of the seven largest economies in the world, was 1%, well below the level at the beginning of the 1960s *(see diagram above left)*.

In this country, inflation is almost exclusively in the service sector of the economy *(see diagram below left)*. The reality is that the prices of goods are now negative and have been flat for the last two years. Anyone in the goods business, from manufacturer or importer through to retailer, is operating in a world where prices are as likely to fall as to rise.

In contrast, in the service sector, inflation has set in. It is much harder to achieve productivity gains in most service industries than it is in manufacturing. This is one of the key reasons why manufacturers are cutting jobs and service industries are increasing them.

In the near future, therefore, we are likely to see increases in the price of services, while prices of manufactured items fall.

G7 Consumer Prices

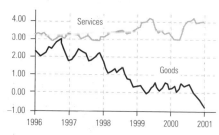

UK Goods and Services Inflation
% Change Over 12 months

Doctor Proctor's DATA QUESTIONS

1 Which sector of the economy has experienced deflation in prices? What does this mean?

2 Why is it more difficult to increase productivity in services than in manufacturing?

3 How might an increase in demand for services help push up the price of services?

4 How might an increase in the supply of goods lower their price?

5 Apart from the UK and USA, list two other countries which are members of the G7 group.

6 Why is inflation likely to continue at very low rates?

7 What might trigger an increase in inflation?

UNIT 3
ACHIEVING ECONOMIC GOALS

Topics covered in this unit

3.1 Economic Tools
The major tools available to achieve economic goals: the interest rate, taxation, government spending, regional policy and exchange rate policy.

3.2 Applying Economic Tools
How can these tools be used in a systematic way to help to secure economic goals? An examination of fiscal policy, monetary policy and exchange rate policy.

3.3 Economic Theory
Introducing the main economic schools of thought: classical, neo-classical, Keynesian, neo-Keynesian, the 'New Economy'.

Questions

In order to achieve economic goals, it is important to be able to apply a set of well-thought-out tools based on sound economic theory. This unit looks at the development and application of modern economic theory.

3.1 ECONOMIC TOOLS

Key Ideas 🔑

Interest Rate Policy

The **interest rate** is the price of borrowing money. In reality, there is not just one interest rate, but a number of different rates available from a variety of different lenders. A key element in determining the interest rate is the risk involved: the higher the risk, the greater the chance of loss by the lender, and therefore the higher the rate.

Although there are many different interest rates, when interest rates rise, they do so across the board. The same applies when they fall.

Doctor Proctor outlines... THE COST OF BORROWING

Most businesses need to borrow money to finance expansion and to fund their day-to-day running. For these businesses, the interest rate is the cost of borrowing money.

In the diagram below you can see what happens when the interest rate falls. The demand for money by business slopes down from left to right. When interest rates fall, the level of borrowing moves from **LB** to **LB¹**.

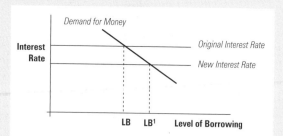

Businesses welcome falling interest rates because they encourage consumers to borrow and spend more. In recent years, borrowing in the UK has increased as a result of low interest rates, as shown in the chart below:

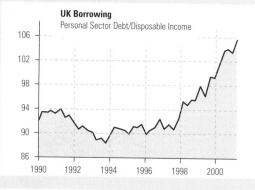

In the UK the interest rate is set each month by the **Monetary Policy Committee** of the Bank of England.

If the economy is growing too quickly the interest rate will be raised; if it is growing too slowly it will be lowered.

The Bank of England's lending rate affects all other interest rates because banks and other financial institutions know that if they need to borrow money themselves they will have to borrow from the Bank of England.

The interest rate charged by banks and building societies is based on the Bank of England's lending rate plus a given percentage, depending on how much profit the bank wants to make from lending and the risk involved in lending.

3.1 ECONOMIC TOOLS

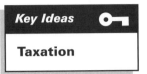

Key Ideas

Taxation

Government levies **taxes** on households and business organisations in order to:

* raise revenue
* discourage certain activities (e.g. smoking, industrial pollution)
* pump extra demand into the economy (in a recession)
* cut excess demand from the economy (when the economy is growing too rapidly).

Taxes on households affect business revenues because they divert money away from expenditure.

Taxes on Households

The two main types of taxes on households are **direct** and **indirect** taxes:

> **Direct** taxes are taken directly away from individuals (e.g. taxes on incomes).

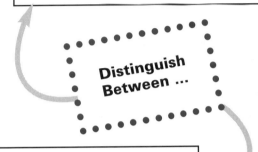

Distinguish Between ...

> **Indirect** taxes are levied on goods and services and on certain types of transaction. For example, VAT is collected by businesses for the government before being passed on in higher prices to the end-consumer.

Doctor Proctor outlines... GOVERNMENT AND LOCAL AUTHORITY TAXATION

The table below shows a breakdown of UK government taxation in the period 2000–2001.

Government Taxation 2000–2001

Taxation	£bn	Type of tax
Income Tax	96	Direct
National Insurance contributions	59	Direct
Excise Duties	37	Indirect
Corporation Tax	34	Direct
VAT	60	Indirect
Business Rate	16	Direct
Council Tax	14	Direct
Other taxes	55	

Businesses will be opposed to taxation if the overall tax burden increases to such an extent that it takes spending out of the domestic economy.

However, they will support a taxation policy that prevents inflation, since inflation can lead to instability and higher wage and overhead costs.

Continued on page 40

3.1 Economic Tools

Doctor Proctor outlines... Government and Local Authority Taxation (Contd)

Income tax
Income tax is generally deducted directly from employees' salaries and paid to the government. Everyone receives a **non-taxable allowance**. Income above this level is taxed at different rates according to level of earnings.

National Insurance
National insurance contributions consist of two elements: an employee's contribution and an employer's contribution. These are deducted directly at the place of work. It is a compulsory insurance scheme for everyone in work and goes to fund important parts of the social security system, such as state pensions. Higher national insurance contributions mean higher production costs for firms.

Corporation Tax
This is a tax on company profits. Smaller firms pay corporation tax at a lower rate. Some items of expenditure can be counted against tax. Businesses argue that corporation tax should be kept to a minimum if business is to survive and to invest in future production.

Value Added Tax
This is a tax on the sale of goods or services. Firms charge VAT to the final customer. The VAT paid by the firm must then be paid over to Customs & Excise. Firms can claim back from Customs & Excise any VAT they have paid on goods they have bought in order to resell.

Excise Duties
Excise duties are taxes on particular goods that are levied for revenue-raising purposes. Examples include duties on beer and cider, wine, spirits, tobacco, petrol, vehicle excise duties, air passenger duty and landfill tax. Businesses are often quite hostile to these taxes because the tax burden raises their costs and limits the amount available for investment.

Council Tax
Council tax is paid by householders to the local council to help fund local expenditure. A rise in council tax will have very much the same impact as a rise in income tax by reducing the money in people's pockets, thus leading to a reduction in expenditure on other things.

Business Rate
Business rate is levied on local businesses to pay for local council services. Again, businesses see this as a cost that discourages enterprise.

Business people dislike taxes that raise their costs. Filing tax returns takes up precious time!

3.1 ECONOMIC TOOLS

Key Ideas 🔑

The Budget

The **budget** is the government's statement of its yearly spending and taxation plans.

In November the government sets out its financial plans for the year in a **pre-budget report**. The final budget is presented to the House of Commons in March by the Chancellor of the Exchequer.

The budget speech is eagerly awaited because it outlines changes to taxes, as well as to government spending. The chancellor will announce any new taxes, and changes to existing tax rates.

The budget is an important macroeconomic tool. It helps to shape the economic climate by increasing or reducing the level of aggregate demand and aggregate supply in the economy.

For example, reducing income tax will help to increase spending in the economy by raising aggregate demand. Reducing corporation tax on small businesses will help by raising aggregate supply.

Doctor Proctor outlines... GOVERNMENT SPENDING

The government is the largest spender in the UK economy. In the period 2000–2001 its major areas of expenditure were:

	£bn
Social Security	103
National Health Service	54
Transport	9
Education	46
Defence	23
Debt Interest	28
Industry and Agriculture	15
Law and Order	20
Housing and Environment	14
Other spending	28

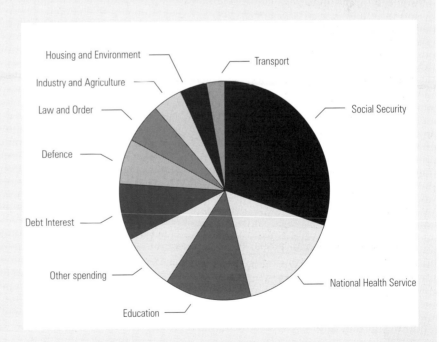

3.1 ECONOMIC TOOLS

Key Ideas 🔑

Government Spending

Doctor Proctor outlines...
TYPES OF GOVERNMENT EXPENDITURE

There are three main types of government expenditure:

1 **Consumption spending** does not involve long-term investment, e.g. teachers' and police salaries, office and administrative supplies for the civil service and government departments.
2 **Capital spending** involves long-term investment, e.g. new police stations and schools, or new jet fighters for the airforce.
3 **Transfer payments** involve the transfer of money from taxpayers to benefit-receivers, e.g. pensions, sick pay, unemployment benefit, etc.

Of the three types of expenditure, capital expenditure is the most likely to contribute to long-term wealth creation.

The government is a major spender because:

1 Some goods would not be provided effectively by the private sector. For example, we have recently seen a loss of confidence in the running of the railway infrastructure system, e.g. lines and signalling, by the privatised rail authority, Railtrack. There are other areas such as health, education, police and defence which need to be provided by government to ensure good-quality long-term provision and not just short-term profit for shareholders.
2 Society needs a safety net for those who cannot afford to buy goods and services themselves.
3 Government is able to influence the level of economic activity in the macro-economy, for example by directly increasing its own level of spending in a period of recession.

Government needs to prioritise areas for improvement in the economy. For example, in recent years the Labour government has given priority to areas such as the police, schools, health and transport.

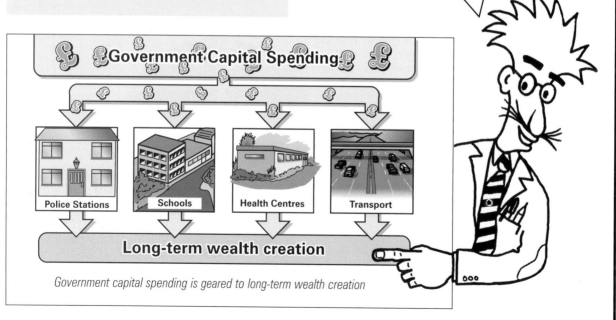

£ £ Government Capital Spending £ £

Police Stations · Schools · Health Centres · Transport

Long-term wealth creation

Government capital spending is geared to long-term wealth creation

3.1 ECONOMIC TOOLS

Key Ideas

Regional Policy

The government uses **regional policy** to address the unequal distribution of wealth and investment in different parts of the UK.

For example, the South East is one of the most successful regions of the UK in attracting new industries and businesses, whereas areas such as Central Scotland, the North West, the North East and the South West have tended to experience much higher levels of unemployment, often resulting from the decline of industries and the reluctance of new industries to set up in these areas.

Over the years regional policy in the UK has included:

- creation of development corporations and 'enterprise zones'
- tax concessions and grants for firms setting up in development areas
- employment subsidies
- location of government offices and administrative centres in areas of high unemployment
- improving communications to areas of high unemployment
- placing of restrictions on businesses setting up in low unemployment areas.

Doctor Proctor outlines... TARGETTING GOVERNMENT ASSISTANCE

The government's regional planning authority identifies areas of the UK which qualify for financial assistance. The European Union also provides regional funds for hard-hit areas of Europe and areas where industry has declined, e.g. those formerly dominated by the iron, steel and coal industries.

Recently the government has recognised that regional inequalities are not as simple as the term 'North/South divide' might suggest, and that there are pockets of prosperity in depressed regions, and pockets of poverty in affluent areas (e.g. some inner London boroughs).

Benefits, subsidies and grants can be seen as having the opposite effects to indirect taxes. Indirect taxes increase costs of production to business, pushing the supply curve to the left. In contrast, subsidies and grants lower the costs of production, pushing the supply curve to the right.

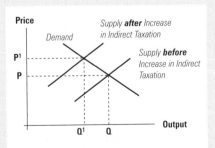

Effect on output of an increase in indirect taxation

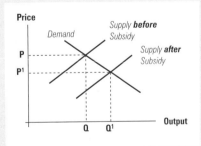

Effect on output of an increase in benefits, subsidies and grants

3.1 ECONOMIC TOOLS

Key Ideas 🔑

Exchange Rate Policy

The **exchange rate** is the rate at which one currency will exchange against other currencies. When a country's currency rises in value, its goods become more expensive abroad.

A country's currency needs to exchange at a high enough rate to bring in healthy revenues from selling goods overseas. If it rises too much, other countries will not want to buy its products. But if the value of a currency falls too much, the country's goods will become so cheap that it may not be worth exporting them at all.

The importance of exchange rates in the competitiveness equation cannot be overstated.

Export-based businesses are often seriously affected by exchange-rate changes, either because their native currency is too strong or because it is too weak.

Doctor Proctor outlines... THE EXCHANGE RATE BALANCE

In order for firms to be competitive abroad, it is essential that the native currency is neither too strong nor too weak. The key is to secure just the right balance: one that makes goods competitive and affordable without being too cheap.

It is also important that exchange rates remain stable over a period of time so that traders know what to expect when they exchange goods.

Government plays a key role in helping to determine exchange rates. The price of the pound in the international marketplace is determined by the demand for, and supply of, pounds. Foreign investors look for strong government and tight control of the economy. A strong UK government will lead to confidence in the pound, which tends to be good for business. A weak government leads to a volatile pound, which is bad for business decision-making.

The value of the pound increases when the country is running a **balance of payments surplus**. This is because more pounds are being bought on international markets to buy UK goods. If UK interest rates are high, this will also push up the exchange rate, as people seek to invest here (hence buying up pounds).

The graph below shows the strength of the pound from the late 1990s to 2001 resulting from the strength of the UK economy, confidence in the British government and the weakness of the Euro.

3.1 ECONOMIC TOOLS

Key Ideas

Fiscal Policy

Fiscal policy is concerned with:

- the way in which the government spends and gathers money to control general levels of economic activity
- the use of the tax system to promote or discourage certain types of activities (e.g. to curb pollution, or to encourage organic farming, etc.).

Through its fiscal policy, the government can also influence the level of demand in the economy by directly altering the amount of its own spending in relation to total tax revenues.

Doctor Proctor outlines... TYPES OF FISCAL POLICY

The government's fiscal stance indicates whether it is trying to expand the economy – that is, to increase employment – or trying to 'take the heat out of the economy' to avoid the risk of inflation.

Its fiscal policy will involve one of the following:

1 A **deficit budget** arises when the government spends more than it takes in taxes. It can then borrow money from banks and other sources, or sell treasury bills and government stock in order to carry out its expenditure policies. The difference between government spending and tax revenue is known as the **Public Sector Borrowing Requirement (PSBR)**.

The logic of the deficit budget is simple: if there is not sufficient spending in the economy to create demand for goods and give everyone a job who wants one, the government can itself boost spending (though this can add to inflation).

2 With a **balanced budget** the government matches its spending with taxes. The idea behind the balanced budget is that the government should not encourage price increases. Some argue that the government itself should spend as little as possible, because private individuals and groups are in a better position to make their own spending decisions.

3 A **surplus budget** arises when the government takes in more revenue than it spends. This can occur if the economy is booming and there is a danger of the economy 'overheating'.

Automatic stabilisers are:

- Taxes which rise as national income rises
- Types of government expenditure that fall as national income rises.

Many **transfer payments** *(see page 42)* fit into this category. For example, when the economy is booming, social security payments will fall. In contrast, when the economy is in a recession, social security payments will be a lot higher, pumping demand back into the economy.

3.2 APPLYING ECONOMIC TOOLS

Key Ideas

Monetary Policy

Dr Proctor says:

'You Must Know This!'

Monetary policy is the deliberate attempt to control:

1 interest rates

2 the money supply

3 credit, i.e. the amount banks can lend to their customers.

The current governor of the Bank of England, Eddie George, has consistently argued that a tight monetary policy is the best way of securing the long-term growth of the economy.

---

1. The Interest Rate

The Bank of England's interest rate is decided by the **Monetary Policy Committee** which meets every month and is made up of bank officials and independent economists. The committee must decide whether the economy is growing too slowly, at the right level, or too quickly. On this basis it decides whether to change interest rates.

At the time of writing, the government has set the MPC a target rate of inflation of 2.5% per annum. Inflation is allowed to fluctuate within 1% of this targeted figure.

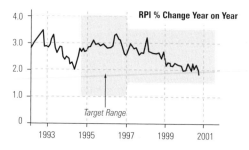

RPI % Change Year on Year

Target Range

In setting the interest rate, the MPC's aim is to keep inflation within government target levels. For example, following the events of September 11th, the MPC lowered interest rates in order to increase demand in the economy as business started to wind down, for example with reductions in air travel and tourism.

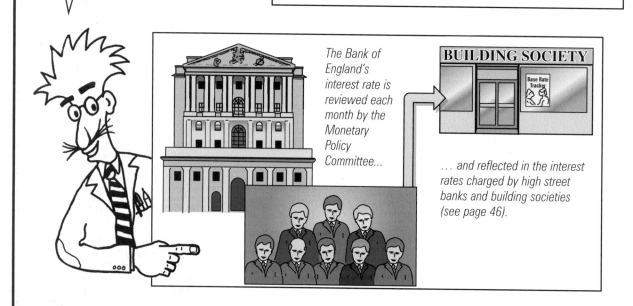

The Bank of England's interest rate is reviewed each month by the Monetary Policy Committee...

BUILDING SOCIETY

Base Rate Tracker

... and reflected in the interest rates charged by high street banks and building societies (see page 46).

3.2 APPLYING ECONOMIC TOOLS

Key Ideas 🔑

Monetary Policy (Contd)

2, The Money Supply

The quantity of money available in the economy is an important determinant of spending. If the government allows the money supply to increase too much, this can lead to inflationary pressures.

The government can reduce the quantity of money that banks have available to lend by selling more treasury bills to the money market. When the government receives cash for these securities, it effectively withdraws money from the financial system.

Reducing the supply of money also pushes up the interest rate because there is a smaller supply of money in the system, as shown below:

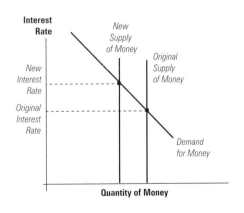

3, Credit

A third form of monetary policy is to control the amount of **credit** that banks and other financial institutions can offer customers. For example, banks can be required to reduce their lending, or the government can make it more difficult for people to buy goods on hire purchase (e.g. by insisting on a larger minimum deposit).

- **Tight** monetary policy involves *raising* interest rates, reducing the quantity of money in the system and making borrowing more difficult.

- **Expansionary** monetary policy involves *lowering* interest rates, increasing the quantity of money in the system and making it easier for people to borrow.

3.3 ECONOMIC THEORY

Key Ideas 🔑

Classical Economics

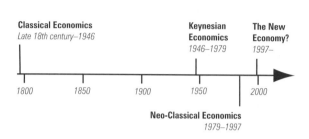

Classical Economics			Keynesian	The New
Late 18th century–1946			Economics	Economy?
			1946–1979	1997–

| 1800 | 1850 | 1900 | 1950 | 2000 |

Neo-Classical Economics
1979–1997

There are many conflicting views about economic priorities and about how best to control and manage economic activity.

Some of the major schools of thought are shown on this timeline.

Doctor Proctor outlines... **ADAM SMITH AND CLASSICAL ECONOMICS**

Adam Smith, 1723–90

Classical economics was developed in the eighteenth and nineteenth centuries when Britain was experiencing an industrial revolution and was spreading its trading empire across the globe.

The ideas of the classical economists were to dominate economic thinking in this country until after the Second World War.

One of the most influential of the classical economists was Adam Smith, whose book *The Wealth of Nations* was published in 1776. Smith argued that the best way to secure the greatest well-being of the community was to allow individuals to pursue their own economic self-interest.

According to Smith, individuals pursuing personal interest and profit could make trades through the marketplace, which acted as an 'invisible hand', guiding the economy to create benefits for all. Smith saw the price system as the mechanism which ensured the efficiency of the marketplace. The government should not get involved in the market because this would reduce its efficiency.

The Profit Motive

According to classical economists, in a free market economy, if people want goods, they will choose them by voting (with their money) for them to be produced. They will also provide labour and other resources to the market, because selling through the market provides them with income to buy goods. Employers will employ labour and other resources so long as they can make a profit.

As goods become old-fashioned or outdated, they are replaced by new goods. Wages fall in some industries and rise in others. Some people will be temporarily unemployed, but they will be taken up in the newer industries. The natural state of affairs for the economy is one of full employment.

According to classical economics, the mass unemployment of the 1920s could be explained by the fact that trade unions and other groups did not allow wages and other prices to fall in a period of recession. If wages and other prices had fallen, employers would have been prepared to employ labour in the new growing industries.

3.3 ECONOMIC THEORY

Key Ideas 🔑

Keynesian Economics

John Maynard Keynes, 1883–1946, argued that government had a role in regulating the operation of the market

The economist **John Maynard Keynes (1883–1946)** developed his theories in order to provide an alternative explanation of the mass unemployment of the 1920s and 30s.

Keynes argued that full employment was just one possible state for the economy. He maintained that the factors that create supply do not always guarantee the same level of demand for goods. Earners of money do not always spend it. A fall in national expenditure will lead to a fall in supply, as suppliers are not able to sell all their stocks of goods. The problem is that aggregate demand is made up of a number of different types of demand, and that the demanders in each case have different motivations.

Doctor Proctor outlines... **AGGREGATE DEMAND: THE KEYNESIAN ANALYSIS**

According to Keynes, **consumer demand** is likely to be determined largely by the level of people's incomes. In a recession many households will start saving because they are worried about losing their jobs (and for other reasons). This leads to a further fall in consumer demand.

Government spending will largely be determined by political factors, as well as the role the government sees itself playing in stabilising the economy.

Exports depend on business competitiveness. They can fall quite quickly if the exchange rate of the pound increases against foreign currencies.

However, **investment** is the most volatile ingredient of aggregate demand. If business people are **confident** that the economy will continue to boom for a period of time, they will be keen to invest. However, if they are gloomy, they will cut back heavily on investment projects.

AGGREGATE DEMAND
- Consumer Demand
- Investment Demand
- Government Demand
- Exports
→ OUTPUT

If you watch business news programmes, you will frequently hear references to **business confidence**.

3.3 ECONOMIC THEORY

Key Ideas

The Multiplier Effect

According to Keynes, changes in demand factors can have a dramatic impact which is **multiplied** several times.

For example, when a building contractor loses a contract to build a new plant, he or she may have to lay off workers. As a result, these workers do not earn wages. They buy less in local shops. The local shops then 'feel the pinch'. They buy in fewer stocks and reduce staff overtime. In turn, these people have smaller incomes and they spend less.

Here is a simple rule for the multiplier effect:

- The greater the percentage of any fresh increase in demand that is leaked away (in savings, imports, and indirect taxes), the smaller the multiplier effect will be.

- The smaller the percentage of any fresh increase in demand that is leaked away (in savings, imports and indirect taxes), the greater the multiplier effect will be.

Doctor Proctor outlines... BEYOND KEYNESIAN ECONOMICS

While Keynesian economics was useful in counteracting unemployment, it did not provide an answer to inflation, which became a major economic problem in the 1970s. In fact, Keynesian policies in some ways added to inflation, because the government tried to spend its way out of recession, pushing prices up still further.

The Neo-Classical Revival
After 1979, when the Conservatives under Margaret Thatcher came to power, there was a significant switch in economic policy away from government-controlled demand-side economics and back to market forces.

A major weakness of the way in which Keynes's ideas had been applied was that successive governments in the 1960s and 70s had used government money to support declining industries. Instead of inefficient units being cut, they continued to survive on government subsidies.

This meant that the UK increasingly lost competitive edge in world markets. National output (the supply of goods) rose very slowly in the 1960s and 70s because supply was rising slowly. An increase in demand tended to lead to both rising prices and an increased reliance on foreign imports. Too many imports led to an increasing national debt.

Britain experienced **stagflation** – a stagnant economy that was not growing, coupled with inflation. Demand management did not seem to be working.

3.3 ECONOMIC THEORY

Key Ideas 🔑

Thatcher, Lawson and the Neo-Classical Revival

During the 1980s, the Conservative government under Margaret Thatcher introduced a raft of neo-classical economic policies aimed at reducing state interference and removing obstacles to the operation of the free market. Nigel Lawson, the chancellor of the time, argued that 'least government is best government'.

Under Margaret Thatcher, government economic policy was aimed at removing obstacles to the supply side of the economy.

The overall effect of this neo-classical revival was to make the market in this country more efficient again.

Prior to 1979, government had tended to 'crowd out' private-sector investment by borrowing much of the available finance capital in the market at higher rates of interest than the private sector could afford.

After 1979, with its privatisation programme under way, the government needed less capital itself. The result was that investment funds were available to be borrowed by more efficient private industries.

The positive result of the neo-classical revival was that the supply side of the economy became more efficient. Growth rates were higher in the 1980s and 1990s, and inflation was also reduced substantially as the money supply was brought under control.

Doctor Proctor outlines... CONSERVATIVE ECONOMIC POLICY

Thatcherite economic policy of the 1980s included:

- Privatising industries – taking them out of 'inefficient' state control

- Removing subsidies from loss-making industries

- Reducing income tax to encourage people to work harder

- Reducing taxes on company profits

- Reducing benefits to those out of work

- Reducing the size of the civil service

- Reducing government spending

- Passing laws to curb trade union powers

- Taking measures against monopolies and restrictive practices

- Encouraging competition amongst groups such as solicitors and opticians and in the health service and in schools.

3.3 ECONOMIC THEORY

Bill Gates, chairman of the US software giant Microsoft: one of the driving forces behind the 'New Economy' of the late twentieth century

Following the general election of May 1997, the Labour government under Tony Blair continued to encourage market forces to flourish.

However, not all New Labour's policies have earned the approval of neo-classical economists.

Examples include the introduction of the minimum wage and the 48-hour working rule which established maximum hours that people could be made to work.

In 2001, Labour also took the privatised Railtrack out of the private sector, making it no longer accountable to shareholders.

The closing years of the twentieth century, saw the economy transformed, not by the deliberate actions of government, but by the high-tech industries, by breakthroughs in science and technology, and by a computer-based network economy driven by rapid communications.

In particular, the US economy experienced a continuous boom throughout the 1990s which was fuelled by giant corporations such as Microsoft.

Doctor Proctor outlines... BLAIRITE ECONOMIC POLICY

The Labour government was fortunate to take over the reins of office during a period of rapid technological development, low unemployment and high productivity – characteristics of the so-called **'New Economy'** (see page 93). However, New Labour's intelligent policies have ensured that it has made the most of its opportunities.

Under Tony Blair, the government has followed an agenda of modernisation involving the development of close links between government and business to generate new jobs in the economy. In particular, the government's monetary policy has been

successful in keeping inflation down – an essential requirement for business confidence.

The government has also put a strong emphasis on the need for the unemployed to take responsibility for themselves in the labour market. At the same time it has worked with business to create a **New Deal** policy that provides work for young and other unemployed workers through the creation of subsidised jobs.

Economic Tools

Interest Rate

What is likely to happen to the rate of interest in the market if the supply of money increases?

Taxation

i) Which of the following are **direct** and which are **indirect** taxes?

- Taxes on wines and spirits
- Income tax
- VAT
- Corporation tax
- National insurance
- Taxes on cigarettes
- Council tax.

ii) What is the name of the tax on business profits?

Government Spending

i) What are the three major areas of government spending?

ii) Which is more likely to lead to an increase in the long-term wealth of the nation: transfer payments made by government or government capital spending?

Regional Policy

List three ways in which government can help economically deprived regions.

The Exchange Rate

What is likely to happen to the value of the Euro when the European Union is running a balance of payments surplus?

Applying Economic Tools

Fiscal Policy

What are **automatic stabilisers**?

Monetary Policy

What are the three main weapons of monetary policy? How might they be used during a downturn in the trade cycle?

Exchange Rate Policy

In the spring of 2002 many British manufacturers complained that the pound was overvalued, making it difficult for them to sell their goods in international markets.

Imagine an alternative scenario in which the pound keeps falling in value against the Euro, the dollar and other major currencies. How might the fall in the value of the pound over time lead to inflation in this country?

Economic Theory

Classical Economics

How does a free market enable consumers to get what they want?

Keynesian Economics

What is the traditional Keynesian recipe for dealing with large-scale cyclical unemployment?

The 'New Economy'

How does the New Economy compare with a stagnant economy characterised by large-scale unemployment and rising prices?

Comparing Economic Theories

Read the following statements and state whether you most closely associate them with:

a) Classical economics
b) Keynesian economics
c) The 'New Economy'.

i) Supply always creates its own demand, so there should never be any long-term unemployment.

ii) Technology in the twenty-first century is helping to drive down costs and create high employment with low inflation.

iii) The economy does not always automatically find the full employment level. Government therefore needs to intervene to make the market work better.

iv) Least government is best government.

v) Government intervention can iron out variations in demand in the trade cycle.

vi) Technology is creating prosperity and providing the answers to economic problems.

vii) The free market is the best solution to creating economic solutions to human problems.

viii) Capitalism needs to be helped if it is going to work smoothly.

ix) Today we are experiencing a revolution akin to the First Industrial Revolution in which costs are continually being driven down and growth driven up.

x) Demand management is an essential function of government.

xi) The best solutions to problems result from the natural laws of the market rather than government interference.

The data in this question is designed to draw together some of your learning from Unit 3.

Bank of England's Monetary Policy Committee Uncertain Over Interest Rates

In January 2002, members of the Bank of England's Monetary Policy Committee were split over whether to lower interest rates, raise them or leave them constant.

At the time, the rate was 4.0% – its lowest level for 38 years. The employers' organisation, the Confederation of British Industry (CBI), was calling for a cut in interest rates to prevent mass redundancies. With the pound high and demand falling after September 11th, businesses were being forced to make cutbacks.

The bank's dilemma was sharpened by fresh figures showing consumer spending levels still high, even as manufacturers revealed plans to cut 15,000 jobs a month. The danger was that a continued rise in consumer spending could lead to inflationary pressures, with low interest rates encouraging more borrowing. House prices had started to pick up,

fuelled by low interest rates for borrowers. Retail sales, household borrowing and house prices were all strong. Some members of the MPC were worried that the low interest rates were encouraging people to build up unsustainable levels of debt.

The CBI urged the bank to cut rates. The latest CBI survey showed that manufacturers were cutting prices at their second-fastest rate since 1958. Together with falling orders and output, this meant that profit margins were coming under intense pressure, forcing businesses to cut jobs and investment. The survey also showed that manufacturers were planning to cut back on training in order to reduce costs. In January 2002 inflation levels were well below the target rate of 2.5%, and in the goods sector there was price deflation.

Doctor Proctor's DATA QUESTIONS

1 What is the MPC? Why was it set up?
2 How might a reduction in interest rates help business?

3 What are the main arguments for a cut in interest rates?
4 Why might the MPC need to be cautious in cutting back interest rates?

UNIT 4

GOVERNMENT AND THE PRIVATE SECTOR

This unit explores the relationship between the public and private sectors of the economy and examines the case for state versus private ownership.

4.1 PUBLIC AND PRIVATE

Key Ideas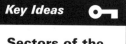

Sectors of the Economy

The economy is made up of two main sectors:

- The **public sector** is owned by the government
- The **private sector** is owned by private individuals and organisations.

	Private Sector	Public Sector
Ownership and control	Owned and run by private individuals	Owned and run by the state on behalf of the taxpayer
Types of organisation	<ul><li>Sole trader (1 owner)</li><li>Partnership (2 or small number of owners)</li><li>Private company (owned by private shareholders – shares not available on Stock Exchange)</li><li>Co-operative – ownership shared among a number of co-operators</li><li>Public company (owned by shareholders, with shares traded on the Stock Exchange)</li><li>Franchise – franchising company sells a franchise to franchisee.</li></ul>	<ul><li>Public corporation (nationalised industry)</li><li>Municipal enterprise (local enterprise)</li></ul>
Aims	<ul><li>profit</li><li>growth</li><li>increased market share</li><li>rewards to individuals.</li></ul>	<ul><li>to provide essential public services</li><li>to use resources well for the benefit of the public.</li></ul>

The chart shows some of the different aims and objectives of the public and private sectors. But don't forget that both the Blair government and the previous Conservative government have stressed the need for the public sector to operate on commercial lines.

4.2 THE CASE FOR PRIVATE OWNERSHIP

Key Ideas 🔑

The Profit Motive

Adam Smith, who wrote his famous book *The Wealth of Nations* in 1766, is considered to be the founding father of classical economics *(see page 48)*.

Smith was primarily concerned with how societies generated wealth. For him, the propulsive force that puts society on an upward growth path is the 'desire for betterment' – or the **profit motive**. This 'impels every manufacturer to expand his business in order to increase profits'.

> The case for private ownership is that it leads to the most efficient use of resources.
>
> Although the Labour Party is historically committed to social ownership, the current Labour government has strongly argued the case for the free market in its White Paper on International Competition in 2001.

Doctor Proctor outlines... MARKET-LED GROWTH

Market-led growth is sometimes described as an engine providing a **propulsive** force. The tracks on which it runs serve as a self-correcting mechanism enabling growth to take place.

At the same time **competition** between producers in the marketplace keeps prices down and ensures that goods are produced in line with consumer requirements.

The classical economists believed that this system worked most efficiently when private entrepreneurs were left to their own devices. They believed that government should stay out of economic decision-making wherever possible.

Government Waste
Governments create inefficiencies because they can only 'second-guess' the wishes of consumers and businesspeople.

For example, if I have £50 in my pocket, I know how spending that £50 will give me the greatest satisfaction. If the government takes £50 from me in tax and then re-spends it on my behalf, it may spend the £50 wisely on my behalf but is unlikely to spend it in a way that fully anticipates my desires.

In addition, the government is likely to be wasteful because of the sheer cost of administration (e.g. civil servants have to be paid wages to collect and spend government money).

THE PRO£IT EXPRESS

4.3 THE CASE FOR STATE CONTROL

Key Ideas

The Public Sector

The **public sector** in the UK is made up of central government, local government and government enterprises such as public corporations.

Central government is responsible for about three-quarters of all government spending and, as we saw earlier, for key items of expenditure such as social security, education and health. In addition the government can, and does, take responsibility for some industries.

Nationalisation means taking an industry or part of an industry into public ownership.

The most common form of nationalised industry in this country has been the **public corporation**.

Doctor Proctor outlines... **THE STRUCTURE OF A PUBLIC CORPORATION**

A **public corporation** has an independent chair and managers who are chosen by the **secretary of state** (a government minister) responsible for that industry.

The day-to-day running of the industry is the responsibility of the chair, although the government minister is responsible for major decisions of a long-term nature – e.g. to close down nuclear power stations.

There are a number of checks and balances to make sure that the industry works in the public interest, e.g. consumers' committees, select groups of MPs with responsibility for the industry, etc. The performance of a nationalised industry is also discussed in the House of Commons at least once a year.

Examples of nationalised industries established in the postwar period include:

- British Steel
- British Coal
- British Rail
- The public utilities, e.g. the water, gas and electricity companies.

Today, there are very few examples of nationalised industries, since most were privatised during the 1980s and 1990s (see chart).

Date	Private Sector	State Sector
1945	Commercially-run coal, steel, rail, gas and electricity supply industries	Key industries taken into public ownership by post-war Labour government
1979	Nationalised industries returned to private sector by Thatcher government	
1997		

Period of Nationalisation (1945–1979)

Period of Privatisation (1979–1997)

Government direct ownership of industry is now largely out of fashion in this country, although the government may step in to protect the public interest.

4.3 THE CASE FOR STATE CONTROL

Key Ideas 🔑

Public Service Organisations

A good example of a modern public corporation is the BBC (British Broadcasting Corporation), which is owned by the government and paid for out of viewers' and listeners' licence fees, as well as from a state grant. The BBC has a number of objectives, including:

'to nurture and cherish the rich diversity of the UK's heritage, identity and cultural life; bringing people together for moments of celebration, common experience and in times of crisis'.

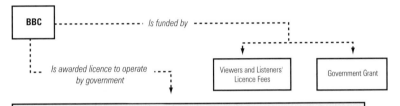

BBC - - - - - - - - - - - - - - - Is funded by - - - - - - - - - - -

Is awarded licence to operate by government

Viewers and Listeners' Licence Fees

Government Grant

OBJECTIVES

Public Service
- Meeting Broadcasting Needs of the Nation
- Maintaining Reputation for Accurate, Impartial Reporting and High-Quality Programming
- Providing Service to Minority Communities and the Regions

Commercial
- Efficient Use of Resources
- Competing in Global Entertainment Market
- Responding to Changing Consumer Demand
- Embracing New Technology

Doctor Proctor outlines... ADVANTAGES OF STATE CONTROL

1 The state can take a long-term view. Whereas private-sector industries may be more concerned with providing high returns to shareholders in the short term, the state can plan 10, 20, 30 years ahead, or even longer.

2 The state is most likely to consider the needs of *all* stakeholders, rather than just shareholder interests.

3 A government monopoly can cut out wasteful duplication. For example, in Victorian times private railway companies often provided more than one railway line to the same destination.

4 The state can run services which are uneconomical to the private sector, e.g. providing a ferry and postal service to remote islands and villages.

5 Many people feel that the state has a responsibility to protect jobs and key industries, even if this means lower profits. Government may also want to protect industries which are important to the UK economy.

4.4 WHY PRIVATISE?

Key Ideas 🔑

Privatisation

Since 1979, a number of public corporations have been **privatised**. This means that they have been sold from the public sector to the private sector and are now owned by shareholders.

A Brief History of Privatisation ...

Mrs Thatcher wins the election and becomes conservative Prime Minister. There are 3m shareholders.

Many industries were public corporations. The Conservatives sold off many of these industries to private shareholders.

When Mrs Thatcher left office, there were 11m shareholders.

The Labour government under Tony Blair has kept these industries in the private sector (with the exception of Railtrack).

Doctor Proctor outlines... THE CASE FOR PRIVATISATION

1 Some people argue that state-run firms are not efficient because they do not have any real competition. They are also protected from bankruptcy, because the government always pays their debts.

2 It is argued that in a modern society as many people as possible should have shares in businesses. The idea is that everyone should become a shareholder, not just the very rich.

3 Privatising industries raises large sums of money for the government. This reduces the government's need to tax people and to borrow money.

Company	Date of Sale	Proceeds (£m)
BP	1979–90	5,723
British Telecommunications	1984, 1991, 1993	17,604
British Gas	1986, 1990	7,793
British Steel	1988	2,425
Regional Electricity Companies	1990	7,997
Electricity Generating Companies	1991	2,969

Dates and proceeds of some of the major privatisations during the period 1979–91

Regulating Privatised Industries

When industries are privatised the government appoints a body called a **regulatory authority**, headed by a **regulator** who is responsible for making sure that the industry runs in the public interest. The regulators must make sure that the industry is efficient and does not charge too much for its services.

4.5 MAXIMISING EFFICIENCY

Key Ideas 🔑

Efficiency

The term **efficiency** in economics is used to describe how well resources are allocated to meet the needs and wants of consumers.

In terms of **productive efficiency** (*see below*), the case for state production is that, as a single monopoly producer, e.g. of coal or rail services, the state is able to benefit from considerable

economies of scale – e.g. in purchasing steel rails, or in buying tea and coffee in bulk for a train restaurant service. Wasteful duplication is also avoided – for example, having two postal services to the same village.

However, **diseconomies of scale** also arise. For example, a state-run industry may be too big to be administered and run efficiently.

There are also what we call **x-inefficiencies** associated with state industries, e.g. employees taking advantage of job security associated with a public service ethic to work less hard than they would in a competitive environment.

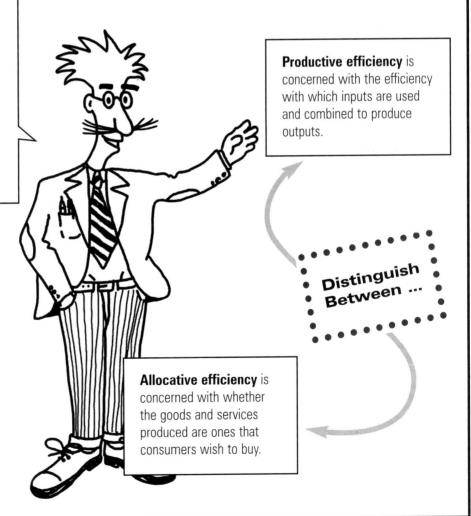

In terms of **allocative efficiency**, a major weakness of state provision is that it limits consumer choice. For example, children may not have a choice of school; patients may not be able to choose in which hospital to have an operation.

Productive efficiency is concerned with the efficiency with which inputs are used and combined to produce outputs.

Distinguish Between ...

Allocative efficiency is concerned with whether the goods and services produced are ones that consumers wish to buy.

Read the following information and then answer the questions below.

Third Way is 'Flaky at the Edges', says Stephen Byers

With the privatisation of the rail network in the mid-1990s, the Thatcher government separated responsibility for rail infrastructure (e.g. track, signalling and equipment) from the operation of train services. Previously, both functions had been the responsibility of a single public corporation, the nationalised British Rail. After privatisation, Railtrack owned the rail network and was responsible for maintaining track, signalling, bridges, viaducts, tunnels, stations and other property, while train services were provided by separate, commercially-operating franchisees.

In the years that followed, there was heated debate about the rights and wrongs of operating the railways for private gain. Accidents such as the Paddington rail disaster of 1999 led some people to argue that Railtrack was cutting corners, particularly in the area of safety, and that safety was being sacrificed to profitability. However, those in favour of privatisation argued that the service was more reliable, and that, taken as a whole, the railways had an excellent safety record.

In 2001/2002 matters came to a head when the transport minister Stephen Byers put Railtrack into receivership, arguing that the state should no longer have to contribute large subsidies while private shareholders were making profits from it. In interviews with the media, Byers claimed that Labour had learned lessons from the Railtrack saga and needed to be more 'hard-edged' in its dealings with the private sector. While the Third Way was plausible in theory, it needed to be tested 'in the cauldron of being in government.' Byers went on: 'I think those principles are still valid. However, it has meant that some of the softer edges of the Third Way have been shown to be flaky'.

Byers announced that Railtrack would be replaced by a not-for-profit company. 'What we've got to do is to be as robust in dealing with the failed private sector as we would be in dealing with a failing public sector.' He described his decision on Railtrack as 'the first major rolling-back on the Thatcher/Major legacy on privatisation that we've seen.'

Doctor Proctor's DATA QUESTIONS

1 What is meant by privatisation? Who were the owners of Railtrack?

2 What were the dangers associated with privatising the railways?

3 How does the failure of Railtrack put into question some of the ideas of the Third Way?

4 What is a not-for-profit company? How might this provide a solution to the problems of Railtrack?

Unit 5

Production, Profit and Distribution

Topics covered in this unit

This unit describes the four main factors of production – land, labour, capital and enterprise – and explains how rewards are distributed to them.

5.1 FACTORS OF PRODUCTION

Key Ideas

Land, Labour, Capital and Enterprise

Economists use the term **factors of production** to identify the four main inputs into production:

- **Labour** – the physical and mental contributions of the workforce to production, e.g. a worker operating a lathe, or a designer designing a new piece of equipment.

- **Land** – all natural inputs into the production process, e.g. land, natural deposits of minerals, fish in the sea, etc.

- **Capital** – plant, machinery and other items of capital used in production. Physical capital is purchased from the money capital invested in the business.

- **Enterprise** – the willingness of the entrepreneur to take the financial risk involved and to bring together the other factors of production, e.g. shareholders and other business owners.

Labour earns **Wages**

Land receives **Rent**

Capital receives **Interest**

Enterprise is rewarded with **Profit**

Labour, land, enterprise and capital – The four main inputs to the production process

5.2 REWARDS TO FACTORS OF PRODUCTION

Key Ideas

Economic Rent

Each of the factors of production described on page 66 needs to be rewarded for inputs into the production process.

But what are their rewards? How are they distributed? What determines how much each of the factors of production will earn?

Doctor Proctor outlines... TRANSFER EARNINGS AND ECONOMIC RENT

In order to attract a factor of production to work for *me* rather than for someone else, I need to pay that factor *at least* the opportunity cost of what it could earn elsewhere.

For example, if I want a bank to lend money to finance my business, and the market rate of interest is 5%, I will need to pay a rate of interest of *at least* 5%.

Economists use the term **transfer earnings** to describe the opportunity cost. In this case the transfer earning is 5% (what the money could earn if it was transferred to its next-best use).

The term **economic rent** is used to describe any reward a factor earns *over and above* its transfer earnings.

The terms **transfer earnings** and **economic rent** can be applied to any factor of production.

The term **economic rent** was first used by the economist David Ricardo to explain the concept of surpluses to landlords. Ricardo showed that because land was in fixed supply, increases in demand would drive up economic rent.

Example

David Beckham earns £80,000 a week playing for Manchester United. The highest salary he could earn elsewhere would be £75,000 a week playing for Arsenal. So:

Beckham's Wage = £80,000 (per week)

Transfer Earning = £75,000 (per week)

Economic Rent = £5,000 (per week)

In the diagram *(left)* the shaded box represents the economic rent resulting from a rise in the demand for land.

In the same way, David Beckham *(above)* can earn a high economic rent, because there is only one David Beckham!

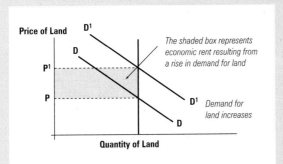

Price of Land

The shaded box represents economic rent resulting from a rise in demand for land

Demand for land increases

Quantity of Land

5.3 WAGE LEVELS IN THE MARKET

Like other costs, the **cost of labour** (wages) is determined by the laws of supply and demand. Labour that is in short supply is able to earn an economic rent relative to the maximum amount it could earn elsewhere.

As the demand for labour increases, so too will wages.

The illustration *(right)* shows how the demand for teachers has increased because of a rise in the number of children at school (i.e. demand has moved from **DD** to **D'D'**).

As a result, teachers' wages have increased.

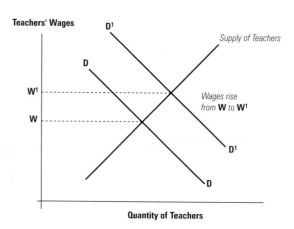

As the supply of labour increases, wages fall, and hence also economic rent. The illustration *(right)* shows what happens to the wages of business studies teachers as more business studies degrees are awarded, and more trained business studies teachers become available for employment.

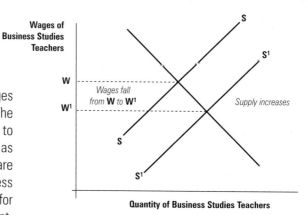

5.3 WAGE LEVELS IN THE MARKET

Key Ideas 🔑

The Role of Trade Unions

A **trade union** is an association of employees formed to protect and promote the interests of its members and to achieve other jointly agreed aims.

Dr Proctor says:

'You Must Know This!'

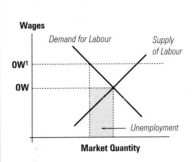

If trade unions push wages up above the market rate, this can lead to a reduction in the number of people employed. If the minimum wage imposed by the trade union is above the market clearing rate, it can stop the market from clearing, leading to higher levels of unemployment.

In the illustration above, **OW** is the market clearing wage rate in the market for labour. However, trade unions have been able to push up wages to **OW¹**. This leads to a fall in employment.

The effect here is similar to that of the government creating a minimum wage which is above the market clearing rate.

However, one reason for introducing a minimum wage is to encourage more people to supply their labour to the market.

Doctor Proctor outlines... WAGES AND PROFIT

For most businesses, wages are the largest single cost of production. The higher the wages it has to pay, the more difficult it is for a business to make a profit.

For example, many people believe that the wages of top footballers are too high. The table *(right)* shows the difficulty faced by Premier League Football clubs in making a profit in 2001 because of the high percentage of their turnover (sales) which had to be paid out in wages.

Club	Total Wages £m	% of Total Turnover	Profit/Loss £m
Arsenal	33,970	56%	+ 21
Aston Villa	24,880	63%	+ 3
Blackburn	22,133	86%	− 20
Bolton	9,238	68%	− 2
Charlton	10,994	86%	− 6
Chelsea	(--- Figures not available ---)		− 10
Derby	17,547	81%	− 8
Everton	19,780	71%	− 10
Fulham	10,917	69%	− 12
Ipswich	8,511	86%	3
Leeds	43,329	50%	− 4
Leicester	22,100	75%	− 6
Liverpool	40,107	86%	3
Man Utd	44,791	35%	21
Middlesbrough	20,056	72%	− 14
Newcastle	28,869	64%	− 20
Southampton	17,290	60%	− 1
Sunderland	23,000	50%	3
Tottenham	26,174	55%	2
West Ham	25,126	70%	− 2

5.4 THE DEMAND FOR AND SUPPLY OF CAPITAL

Key Ideas

Business Confidence

Unlike other factors of production, the market for capital is significantly affected by **business confidence**. When investment decisions are made, it is not possible to predict exactly what the return will be. An investment in a state-of-the-art high-tech application may turn out to have a low return because technology moves on.

Each month a survey is carried out into **business confidence** in the UK. The level of optimism will influence the level of business investment. If business people think that the economy is about to boom, they will be much more likely to invest than if they think a recession is round the corner.

Doctor Proctor outlines... MARGINAL EFFICIENCY OF CAPITAL

Expected returns on investment can be shown in a graph known as the **Marginal Efficiency of Capital** curve. The curve slopes down from left to right because the first investment projects to be taken up are always those with the highest returns. The greater the level of investment, the lower the rate of returns on later projects.

The term **marginal** refers to the extra amount of capital invested. You can see that each extra amount of capital invested is expected to yield a smaller return.

The quantity of investment that takes place depends on the relationship between the marginal efficiency of capital and the rate of interest, which is the cost of borrowing for investment purposes.

The diagram below shows the quantity of investment that would take place at an interest rate of 5%.

If the interest rate is increased from 5% to 6%, this will reduce the number of investment projects and also reduce the economic rent to capital:

5.5 ENTERPRISE AND PROFIT

Key Ideas 🔑

Normal and Supernormal Profit

Economists make a distinction between **normal** and **supernormal profit**:

Normal profit is the minimum level of profit required for a business to commit itself to a type of business or production – in other words the opportunity cost of carrying out a particular type of business/production.

It is easy to understand why it is important for businesses to earn supernormal profit. Shareholders will be much more tempted to invest in a company with a high shareholder return than one with a low shareholder return (although shareholders are often influenced by factors other than pure profit – for example, whether or not the company operates in an ethical way).

Distinguish
Between ...

Supernormal profit is the profit earned *over and above* normal profit.

Example

A website designer can make *either* £5,000 profit a year from setting up in Walsall, *or* £6,000 profit a year from setting up in Birmingham.

If she chooses to set up in Birmingham:

- **normal** profit will be £5,000 per year (the opportunity cost of setting up in Walsall);

- **supernormal** profit will be £1,000.

Supernormal profit is thus a form of economic rent.

5.6 WHO BENEFITS?

Key Ideas

Distribution

Distribution refers to the sharing out of the rewards of economic activity. One of the key economic questions is that of 'who benefits'?

Doctor Proctor outlines... INEQUALITY: FOR AND AGAINST

In most businesses, labour receives about 70% of income in the form of wages. However, it is important to remember that income and wealth are very unevenly distributed in the UK and other market-driven economies.

Richer people are likely to receive income from several sources, e.g. wages, interest, profit and rent. Those in favour of the market system argue that inequalities act as an incentive for hard work and investment. They see taxes and benefits as disincentives to hard work and enterprise.

Those opposed to the free market argue for a more equitable distribution of income so that everyone is able to benefit from living in an advanced industrial society.

Equity and Value Judgements

The concept of equity involves **value judgements**. The Conservative government under Margaret Thatcher believed that everybody should benefit from rising incomes. However Margaret Thatcher also saw inequality as a necessary spur to motivate people to work harder and better themselves.

In contrast, Karl Marx set out his beliefs about equity as follows:

'From each according to his ability – to each according to his need.'

Factors of Production

Classify the following into land, labour, capital and enterprise:

- oil reserves
- oyster beds
- skilled car-fitters
- shareholders
- a business owner
- machinery
- an oil rig
- a roadsweeper
- a machine tool
- a teacher
- a franchisee for a takeaway pizza outlet

Rewards to Factors of Production

If a piece of land yields £100,000 worth of potatoes and it could earn £70,000 from growing turnips and £50,000 from sunflowers:

a) How much economic rent is yielded from growing potatoes?

b) What is the transfer earning from the land?

Wage Levels in the Market

1 Use demand and supply analysis to explain why doctors earn more than nurses.

2 Use demand and supply analysis to show how an increase in the number of foreign nurses coming into the UK is likely to affect nurses' wages.

3 The graph below shows the demand for and supply of cleaners employed in the UK. If the government sets a minimum wage at **0W**, what will be the impact on the number of cleaners employed in the UK?

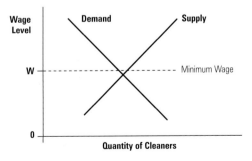

The Demand for and Supply of Capital

The diagram below shows the number of investment opportunities taken up at an interest rate of 10%. What would happen to the number of investment opportunities taken up if the interest rate falls to 5%?

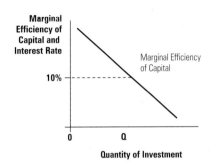

Enterprise and Profit

A monopoly firm makes abnormal profits of £250,000 per year. These profits encourage new firms to enter the industry. How is this likely to affect the level of profits made by the firm that previously had the monopoly? In the long run why might this firm leave the industry?

Who Benefits?

What is the difference between **equity** and **equality**?

The data in this question is designed to draw together some of your learning from Unit 5.

Gap Grows in Weekly Pay of Highest and Lowest Earners

Official figures compiled by the New Earnings Survey released on January 24th 2002 reveal that the gap between Britain's best-paid and worst-paid workers is growing, and was wider than at any time since Labour came to power in 1997.

The figures show that the top 10% of earners take home at least £722 per week, enjoying an average rise in pay of 7.3%. In contrast, the bottom 10% of workers have enjoyed a much smaller average rise of only 4.5%, leaving them with pay of £207 per week or less – even further behind the biggest earnings.

The best-paid workers in the country in early 2002 thus earn at least 71.3% more than those at the bottom. When Labour came to office the difference was about 70%.

The survey also shows that an increasing number of people – about 320,000 – are taking home less than the minimum wage.

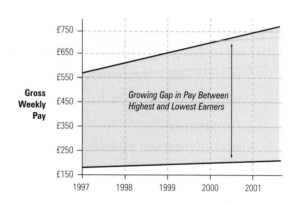

The pay gap between men and women's pay is 18.5%. The best-paying sector was the City, with average weekly pay of £599, followed by mining and quarrying at £567.

Doctor Proctor's DATA QUESTIONS

1	What evidence is provided in the data that some people are earning economic rent? What is economic rent?	3	How would you account for the differences in weekly wages between financial workers in the City and those in other occupations?
2	Is it likely that some people are earning no economic rent?	4	What explanations can you put forward for the differences between men's and women's pay?

Unit 6

Economics of the Firm

Topics covered in this unit

6.1 Costs and Revenues
Fixed and variable costs and the concept of the break-even point.

6.2 Economies of Scale
How large firms are able to produce large outputs at low unit costs. The sources of scale economies.

6.3 The 'Perfect Market'
An ideal model of competition. How competition helps to create allocative efficiency.

6.4 Monopoly
How monopoly firms are able to raise prices and/or limit output.

6.5 Competition among the Few
What happens when a few firms dominate a market? Is this good or bad for consumers?

Questions

This unit looks at ways in which firms compete in different markets. Firms need to cover their costs with revenues and ideally make a profit.

6.1 COSTS AND REVENUES

All businesses incur **costs** in the production process. These fall into two main types:

- **Fixed costs** do not vary with the quantity of output produced or the number of sales made. Examples include salaries paid to production staff, and the costs of heating or lighting an office.
- **Variable costs** vary with the quantity of output produced. They include raw materials (e.g. cocoa in chocolate production) and the wage costs of individual items. (These can be calculated according to how much labour time is required to produce them.)

Example

A business has daily **fixed** costs as follows:

Rent and Rates	£300
Salaries	£500
Other	£200
Total Fixed Costs =	£1,000

These can be spread over the number of units produced. If the business produces only 100 units, fixed costs per unit of output will be high: £10. However, if the firm produces more units, the same fixed costs can be spread over the larger output. If the firm produces 10,000 units of output, the fixed cost per unit will only be 10p.

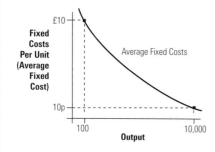

In contrast, total **variable** costs will start at zero and rise according to the level of output produced.

Over a very small output, the variable cost would be high for each unit produced – because at low outputs equipment and machinery could not be used effectively.

As output increases, variable costs per unit will start to fall, because the variable inputs such as labour will be able to work more efficiently with the fixed factors such as machines.

Beyond a certain point, variable factors become less efficient again because they cannot secure any more productivity gains out of working with the existing machinery and equipment.

We can say therefore that, at first, as we add more variable factors to fixed factors, there are **increasing returns**. After a certain point, **diminishing returns** set in, as illustrated by the diagram below:

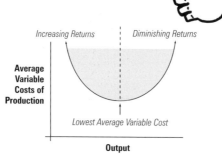

6.1 COSTS AND REVENUES

Key Ideas 🔑

Break-Even Point

We use the term **break-even point** to describe the point at which sales levels are high enough to cover costs, but not high enough to make a profit.

All businesses must cover their costs if they are to survive for more than a short time. Normally businesses are able to cover their costs with the revenues that they receive from sales.

Example

Sunil runs a small business buying, repairing and selling computer parts. His fixed costs are £400 a week. He buys in these parts for £40 each and sells them on at £120 each. How can we illustrate his break-even point?

Customer Numbers	Fixed Cost	Variable Cost	Total Cost	Sales
£	£	£	£	
2	400	80	480	240
4	400	160	560	480
6	400	240	640	720
8	400	320	720	960

Step 1
The first stage is to quantify costs and revenues at different volumes of sales. These figures are shown in the table *(right)*.

Step 2
The next step is to plot Fixed Costs, Total Cost and Sales Revenue against business activity – in this case, the number of computer parts sold.

The point at which the lines for Sales Revenue and Total Cost intersect is the break-even point.

At Sales Volumes to the left of the break-even point, the vertical gap between the Sales and Total Cost lines represents the loss made. To the right of the break-even point, the gap between the two lines represents profit.

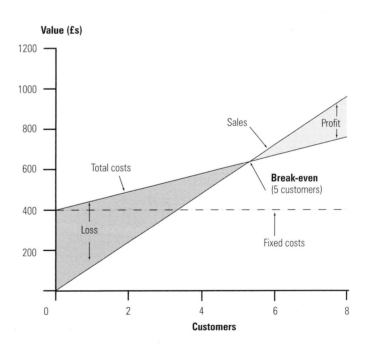

6.2 ECONOMIES OF SCALE

Key Ideas 🔑

Internal and External Economies

Internal economies are those which develop from growth within an individual company.

Economies of scale are simply the advantages that large firms enjoy as a result of their size, enabling them to produce higher outputs at lower costs per unit.

Distinguish Between ...

External economies are advantages to firms resulting from the growth of a whole industry or region.

Example

In 1995 a firm has relatively low fixed costs and reaches its lowest average cost point at a fairly low level of output.

By 2000, the firm has expanded its capacity so that it has greater fixed cost levels but is able to produce larger quantities at lower average cost.

By 2005 it has benefited from economies of scale still further. Its fixed costs are higher but it can produce large outputs at low unit costs.

The illustration shows how a business can benefit from economies of scale over time.

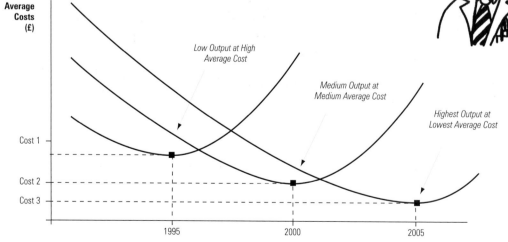

Low Output at High Average Cost

Medium Output at Medium Average Cost

Highest Output at Lowest Average Cost

6.2 ECONOMIES OF SCALE

Internal Economies

There are several sources of internal economies:

1 **Technical economies**. Large organisations use techniques and equipment that cannot be adopted by small-scale producers. For example, a company may have four machines each producing 1,000 units per week at a unit cost of £2. As the company grows, these can be replaced by one machine producing 5,000 units per week at the lower unit cost of £1.

2 **Labour and managerial economies**. In larger organisations, highly skilled workers can be employed full-time in jobs that utilise their specialised skills, without having to be constantly switched from one type of job to another, whereas in a small business unit, workers often have to be 'jacks-of-all-trades'. In the same way, a larger company can employ management specialists, such as accountants, marketing managers and personnel managers.

3 **Commercial economies**. Larger firms are able to purchase raw materials in bulk at a discount. Marketing activities such as advertising and market research can be spread over a large customer base at lower unit costs. Selling operations can also be simplified to reduce costs.

4 **Financial economies**. As larger companies represent a more secure investment, they find it easier to raise finance. They are also frequently treated more favourably by the banks, and are in a better position to negotiate loans with preferential interest rates.

External Economies

External economies of scale occur when an entire industry or region expands and all the individual firms within the industry or region benefit:

1 **Economies of concentration**. A range of special services develops including networks of local suppliers and ancillary trades, and local college courses offering specialised training. The area as a whole may also earn a reputation which benefits individual firms.

2 **Economies of information**. Larger industries can set up special information services to benefit producers, e.g. research units such as The Chemical Research Unit or specialist publications such as *The Building Trades Journal*.

3 **Economies of disintegration**. The term **disintegration** describes the way in which business activity can take place at several locations in different firms, rather than being part of the integrated activity of one firm. Often firms are attracted to areas where specialised industries already exist – for example, companies producing components or offering maintenance and other forms of support. Examples include the many software houses supplying large computer companies in the Thames valley.

6.3 THE 'PERFECT MARKET'

Key Ideas

Perfect Competition

In the real world there is no such thing as a perfect market. But it is possible to imagine a situation in which the laws of supply and demand work perfectly and no producer is able to exploit the consumer.

Doctor Proctor outlines... IMAGINING THE PERFECT MARKET

Economists have defined the conditions for a perfect market as follows:

- **Each version of the product is identical** – so no producer can claim their version is any better than that of their rivals. Advertising is pointless.

- **Many buyers and sellers** – so competition is intense.

- **Consumers have perfect information** – buyers know every price available and will always buy from the cheapest seller.

- **New firms can enter the market immediately** – so any profits made by existing firms are immediately 'competed away'.

In these conditions there is absolutely no possibility of any producer charging a higher price than other sellers. Firms simply make **normal profit** *(see page 71)*.

The nearest real-world examples of a perfect market might be the market for identical agricultural products such as a particular variety and grade of wheat. Another case might be the market for identical items on the internet, where there are many rival buyers, all of whom have access to detailed and up-to-date information about products and prices.

6.4 MONOPOLY

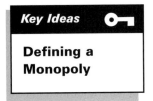

Key Ideas

Defining a Monopoly

A **monopoly** is created when 25% or more of the market for a good or service is controlled by one supplier or seller.

There are various ways in which monopolies can come into existence:

- A **natural monopoly** exists where a natural resource such as a mineral only occurs in one part of the world. For example, most of the diamonds in the world are found either in Russia or Southern Africa.

- The **government** can also create monopolies. For example, only one company has been given the licence to run the National Lottery, and certain companies such as Virgin have been given the franchise to run the railway in selected locations.

- Monopolies also occur when economies of scale are required to run particular industries, and small firms simply cannot compete with very large ones. For example, Corus is the major steel producer in this country, operating huge blast furnaces and rolling mills.

Doctor Proctor outlines... THE CONTROL OF MONOPOLIES

The argument against monopolies is that they make abnormal profits and can also exploit the consumer by restricting output. A monopoly market therefore is not based on **allocative efficiency** *(see page 61)*.

Because of the potential welfare loss of monopolies, they are heavily regulated. In some industries regulators can control annual price increases and introduce fresh competition, in accordance with rules laid down by government.

Problems occur when a market structure becomes monopolistic, e.g. if a merger or take-over causes a firm to supply more than 25% of the market. Such mergers are investigated by the **Competition Commission**.

Cases are referred to the Competition Commission by the **Director General of Fair Trading**. The Competition Commission investigates and reports on cases where monopolistic situations exist or where there are anti-competitive agreements between firms, e.g. where firms collude to fix prices or to restrict supplies.

The Competition Commission needs to weigh up whether or not market situations are against the public interest. Today, UK monopoly legislation must also comply with European Union regulations.

6.4 MONOPOLY

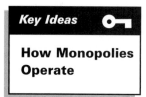

Key Ideas

How Monopolies Operate

A company which has a monopoly is faced with a **downward-sloping demand curve**. This means that if it wants to sell more goods, it will only be able to do so at lower prices (because of the laws of demand).

The monopolist's demand curve can also be called the **average revenue curve** because it shows the average revenue (price) that the company could charge for different quantities that it might want to sell.

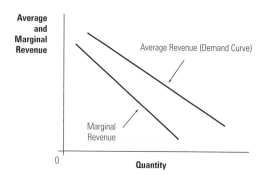

The **marginal revenue curve** lies below the average revenue curve, showing the extra revenue that would be received for selling additional units of the product.

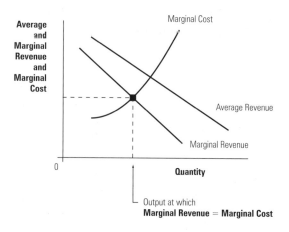

Continued opposite

6.4 MONOPOLY

Key Ideas

How Monopolies Operate (Contd)

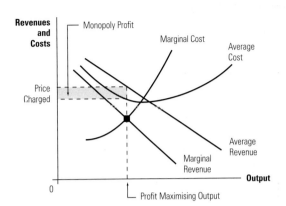

Assuming that a monopolist wishes to maximise profits, it will carry on producing extra units of a good up to the point where the marginal cost of producing an extra unit is equal to the marginal revenue received from selling an extra unit.

In order to show the profit made by the monopolist, we need to plot a typical average cost curve onto the diagram. As we have seen, the monopolist produces where Marginal Cost equals Marginal Revenue. At this point Average Revenue is higher than Average Cost.

The profit made is the Total Revenue minus Total Cost.

This is represented by the shaded area in the diagram.

In other words:

$$\text{Total Revenue} = \frac{\text{Average Revenue} \times}{\text{Quantity Sold}}$$

$$\text{Total Cost} = \text{Average Cost} \times \text{Quantity Sold}$$

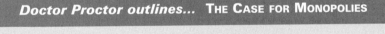

Doctor Proctor outlines... THE CASE FOR MONOPOLIES

Although monopolies can work against the interests of the consumer, there are some arguments in their favour.

1 Monopolies involve economies of scale which can benefit the consumer. For example, very large supermarket chains can buy in bulk and sell at low prices. In other words, there are gains in **productive efficiency** that can be passed on to the consumer.

2 Monopolies also can be heavily involved in **research and development (R&D)**. For example, the pharmaceutical companies in this country argue that they need to make abnormal profits in order to fund research and development of new medicines and cures for the future.

6.5 COMPETITION AMONG THE FEW

Key Ideas

Oligopoly

Oligopoly means 'competition among the few'. It is typical of many markets in the UK today.

These markets may be characterised by intense rivalry between competitors, with each constantly trying to outguess the strategy of the others and borrow ideas from them. Competition may be based on price or other factors such as quality or value-added.

Many of the major markets for consumer goods in the UK involve a relatively small number of firms selling broadly similar products. Often the producers are multinationals such as the Anglo-Dutch Unilever, the American Heinz or the Swiss Nestlé.

Oligopoly markets are likely to be most competitive when there are a number of firms close to the 'market leader' position. The firm that gains **market leadership** is able to undercut rivals by achieving greater economies of scale.

Some oligopoly situations may be less competitive – for example, when firms collectively recognise that aggressive competition is forcing down their prices. There may even be collusion between firms to keep prices above a certain level.

A cartel is an arrangement between a group of firms or countries to fix prices. For example, the Organisation of Petroleum Exporting Countries (OPEC) has often worked toegther to raise prices by restricting the supply of oil .

Examples

Market	Dominated by
Tabloid newspapers	the *Sun*, the *Mirror*, the *Mail*, the *Express*, the *Sport*
Confectionery	Cadbury, Mars, Unilever
Washing powder	Procter & Gamble, Unilever
Supermarkets	Asda, Tesco, Sainsbury
Petrol retailing	Shell, Esso, BP

Tabloids and petrol: competitive markets in which firms sell very similar products

Costs and Revenues

1 Which of the following are variable and which are fixed costs for a chocolate factory?

- Wages which are linked directly to output
- Management salaries
- Rent and rates on premises
- Raw material costs
- Lighting costs in the factory
- Water used directly in the production process

2 A bookshop sells 1,000 books in a month. The average cost of buying books for resale is £5 and the average selling price of books is £10. If the bookshop has fixed costs of £1,000, how many books would it need to sell each month to break even?

Economies of Scale

How do economies of scale enable firms to sell large outputs at lower unit costs?

Give an example of an important economy of scale in the case of a large hotel chain.

A soft drinks manufacturer benefits from a number of economies of scale. Are they **internal** or **external**?

i)   The plant invests in new state-of-the-art technology enabling much longer production runs.
ii) A new supplier sets up close to the firm.
iii) The firm is able to negotiate preferential loans with a bank based on its scale.
iv) The firm engages in a global advertising campaign.
v)   The local university starts running management courses for managers in the soft drinks firm.
vi) The government gives permission for a new airport to be built within five miles of the firm's head office.
vii) The firm is able to arrange discounts for employee training with a national training provider.
viii) A recycling plant is built within the town where the firm's manufacturing plant is located.

The 'Perfect Market'

Why are the following conditions necessary in order for a 'perfect market' to exist?

- An identical product
- Ease of entry for new firms into the industry
- Perfect information available to all consumers.

Monopoly

Copy the diagram below and then shade in the abnormal profit that could be made by the monopolist shown.

Why does allocative efficiency not occur under monopoly conditions?

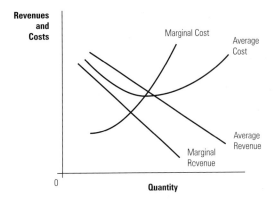

Competition among the Few

Give an example of an oligopoly market other than those already mentioned. How intense is competition in the industry that you have outlined? How do firms compete in this sector?

Which of the following are characteristic of a competitive oligopoly?

i)   A large number of firms compete in the same market.
ii)   Firms produce an absolutely identical product.
iii) New firms are able to enter the market.
iv)   There are relatively few firms in the market.
v)   Products are differentiated.
vi)   Rival firms compete aggressively.
vii) Firms are generally aware of what rivals are doing.
viii) Firms compete through advertising.
ix)   Firms compete to become the market leader.
x)   It is impossible for new firms to enter the industry.
xi)   It is legal for firms to collude in setting prices.
xii) There are very few consumers in the market.

The data in this question is designed to draw together some of your learning from Unit 6.

Amazon Makes a Profit

In the fourth quarter of 2001 the internet book trader Amazon broke into profit for the first time. The profit was fairly modest. A couple of years earlier, many people had predicted massive profits for companies trading through the internet, arguing that costs and prices would be slashed and that large numbers of consumers would be tempted away from traditional retailers.

What many had not reckoned with was the fact that, while people may be able to order books online at a low cost, the distribution costs of getting the books to them on time are high. Because the internet is available to all, consumers are also able to search around for the best prices, making internet book-buying a highly competitive market.

For those who doubted that a business with so few barriers to entry could ever be profitable, Amazon had an answer – first-mover advantage. Whichever company populated the new distribution channel first would have a powerful advantage over late-comers in creating a global brand, and could therefore be expected to 'clean up'.

Of course, for internet traders, one problem is that of having to spend large sums of money on marketing so that people can find out about their products. Setting up an internet venture is very costly in terms of marketing and promotion. This is why a number of internet companies with good ideas have failed. However, it now seems that Amazon.com have got their message across, and that many buyers are using the internet to buy books. Inevitably, traditional booksellers have responded. For example WHSmith has launched its own web-based offshoot, WHSmith.com, to enable customers to purchase books online.

To succeed in the long term, Amazon needs to build up such a large market that it can benefit from larger economies of scale than rivals – holding larger stocks, buying in greater bulk, and cutting distribution costs. However, it will also have to contend with the fact that existing booksellers already have many of these advantages – and strong brand names as well. These established companies simply need to build up a strong internet presence to rival that of Amazon.

Doctor Proctor's DATA QUESTIONS

1   What are the barriers to entry in the internet book trade?

2   What factors determine the level of competition in this industry?

3   What factors are likely to prevent Amazon from making monopoly profits?

4   What is meant by **first-mover advantage**?

5   Is it possible to sustain this advantage over time?

Topics covered in this unit

7.1 Institutional Economics
How social institutions shape the way in which economic decisions take place

7.2 Environmental Economics
Valuing the environment in economic decision-making

7.3 International Economics
The impact of globalisation on the world economy. 'Free' and 'fair' trade

7.4 The 'New Economy'
Competition, the growth of communications technology and their impact on the Western economies.

7.5 The Euro
The importance of the Euro to UK business and the economy

Questions

Economics is a constantly developing field. That is why it is important to look at new ideas and emerging issues such as the impact of the Euro, and the growth of 'New Economy'.

7.1 INSTITUTIONAL ECONOMICS

Key Ideas 🔑

The Social Context of Economic Decisions

Institutional economics was first developed in the early twentieth century.

It emphasises the **social setting** in which economic decisions take place. For institutional economists, economic activity does not take place in a textbook model, but in a real society.

Doctor Proctor outlines... INSTITUTIONAL ECONOMICS

Institutional economists argue that, over time, patterns and behaviours become institutionalised in society. These patterns shape our thinking and thus our laws and social framework. (For example, it is often argued that racism has become **institutionalised** in our society – i.e. that it is an ongoing legacy from the past.)

Early institutional economists showed how institutions placed constraints on individual behaviour. For example, American society was seen as being dominated by relationships based on

money and money-making. Over time, these existing pathways were built upon and new generations took on current values as their own – i.e. progress was **path-dependent**.

Institutional Economics and the Neo-Classical Revival

In recent years, interest in institutional economics has grown, partly as a reaction to the neo-classical revival which took place between 1979 and 1997.

The neo-classical economists used mathematical models to show the benefits of free trade, arguing that market models can and should be applied almost everywhere. This modelling often ignored the existing institutional framework.

For example, from the time of the October Revolution of 1917 until late 2001, it was impossible for Russian citizens to buy and sell land. Institutional economists would argue against the idea of imposing a free-market model on a society which had so little knowledge or experience of how the free market works.

Recently, institutional economists have studied institutional factors such as property rights and governance structures, showing how these affect economic transactions and activities. Their aim has been to reduce petty restrictions that push up costs, to create a more stable legal and commercial framework in markets and to improve social benefits through co-ordinated institutional activity.

The early institutional economist, **Thornstein Veblen**, argued that American institutions did not necessarily lead to social benefit – in fact, the opposite: business interests were about promoting narrow self-interest at the expense of society as a whole.

7.2 ENVIRONMENTAL ECONOMICS

Key Ideas 🔑

Environmental Costs and Benefits

Environmental economics provides another challenge to traditional economic thinking.

Until recently the environment was exploited as a free good. Environmental economists have tried to oppose this by placing a monetary value on the environment. Their approach has been to interview members of the public to find out how much value they place on environmental assets, by asking them 'How much would you be willing to pay to preserve X?'

This **monetisation** of environmental assets helps to provide a basis for **cost–benefit analysis** – for example, when deciding whether or not to build new roads or other projects which have an impact on the environment.

Cost–benefit analysis involves adding together all the costs involved in a project (including environmental costs), and all the benefits (including environmental benefits). The decision to proceed is based on whether the costs outweigh the benefits. For example:

Coming to a rural area near you!!
Greenfield Developments Plc
SHOPARAMA
Retail and Leisure Park

Benefits
- Easy parking
- Wide range of goods
- Job opportunities

Costs
- Environmental pollution
- Traffic congestion
- Loss of town-centre trade
- Loss of rural amenity

Doctor Proctor outlines...LIMITATIONS OF ENVIRONMENTAL VALUATION

In practice, the type of environmental valuation described above has had the effect of raising the value placed on environmental assets. However, many critics claim the exercise is fundamentally flawed.

In their view, the environment cannot be broken down into separate 'assets': it forms an integral whole, and no part of it can be removed or destroyed without affecting the rest.

They also criticise the 'willing to pay' questioning technique, since those questioned know that they will not be expected to part with real money. A better question would be: 'How much would you

be willing to receive *in compensation for the loss of* xyz environmental asset?' Most interviewees would put a much higher value on the environment if questioned in this way. Indeed, some might say: 'I'm not prepared to part with xyz at any price!'

Despite the criticisms, environmental economics has succeeded in promoting new ways of thinking about the environment and has paved the way for government initiatives such as landfill taxes and taxes on the creation of greenhouse gases. Environmental economists have also done important work in creating a rationale for subsidies, particularly for sustainable farming practice.

7.3 INTERNATIONAL ECONOMICS

Key Ideas

Globalisation

In recent years the world has moved from an international to a **global economy**.

Twenty years ago, most large international companies were identified with a particular country, e.g. Nestlé with Switzerland and Heinz with the USA.

Today, the picture is less clear. Large transnational companies have shareholders around the world. Transnational companies have access to global capital and are less accountable

to national governments. The graph below shows how in recent years we have seen a much higher level of capital flow for international investment – particularly amongst advanced economies such as Britain, Japan, the UK and the USA.

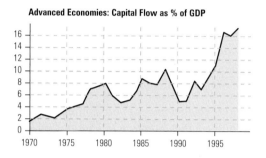

Advanced Economies: Capital Flow as % of GDP

Investment in large transnational companies has risen dramatically in recent years.

Doctor Proctor outlines...THE GLOBAL MARKETPLACE

In the new global marketplace, a handful of powerful brands can dominate entire continents

In a global economy, companies focus on what they do best, concentrating on their 'power brands' e.g. Heinz Baby Foods, Unilever's Magnum ice cream, etc. These companies have the greatest competitive advantage in producing these items, and they can benefit from economies of scale in marketing and distributing them.

Today companies like Unilever and Heinz produce **global products**, i.e. products that are sold in the same form with standardised marketing across the globe. This has contributed to a worldwide convergence of lifestyles and patterns, with the result that teenagers drink Coca-Cola and wear identical Nike caps and trainers in almost every country in the world.

7.3 INTERNATIONAL ECONOMICS

Key Ideas 🔑

The Expansion of World Trade

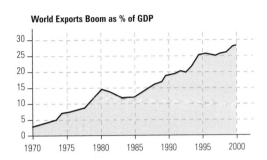

World Exports Boom as % of GDP

Coupled with the globalisation of markets has been a massive **expansion** in the sheer volume of international trade.

Causes have included rising living standards, and the breakdown of divisions between countries, e.g. between Eastern and Western Europe, and the opening up of markets in China and India to international trade.

The **World Trade Organisation (WTO)** has also been particularly successful in progressively reducing trade barriers such as import taxes which inhibit the flow of goods between countries.

Doctor Proctor outlines...FREE TRADE AND FAIR TRADE

Many would say that the expansion of world trade has accentuated the gap between rich and poor.

Critics argue that countries cannot engage in 'fair trade' if they only produce low-value-added products such as raw commodities (e.g. sugar, rubber, crude oil, etc.). These countries are likely to be exploited in the exchange process.

What is needed therefore is **fair trade** rather than **free trade**. Fair trade involves paying a fair price that helps less developed countries to improve their economies, e.g. by investing in better education to improve the intellectual capital of the workforce.

Fair trade
Trade in which goods are exchanged at a fair price rather than for the minimum. Fair trade recognises the social costs and benefits of trading.

Distinguish Between ...

Free trade
Unimpeded trade between countries, with each country specialising in what it does best.

7.3 INTERNATIONAL ECONOMICS

There is fierce debate among economists about whether or not the development of the global economy is a good thing:

- Those in favour of globalisation see it as leading to a rapid rise in living standards in all countries as the benefits of free trade lead to an acceleration in economic growth. The free flow of capital enables new economies to develop.

- Critics argue that the growth of the world economy is very unequal, and that those countries less well endowed with factors of production geared towards the modern economy are bound to lose out. Investors are only interested in countries where they can make high returns.

  The result is that, for example, between 1970 and 2000, one-third of foreign direct investment in the developing world has been in China. Three-quarters of all investment in the developing world has been in Brazil, Mexico, Argentina, Singapore, Malaysia and China. The rest of the developing world has received very little.

Doctor Proctor outlines... TRADE AND SOCIAL RESPONSIBILITY

Nobel prize-winning economist Amartya Sen has argued strongly for a social dimension to world trade

The Nobel prize-winning economist Amartya Sen shares the views of the institutional economists mentioned earlier *(see page 88)*, arguing that trade must be considered within a political and social setting as well as an economic one.

In a competitive world market based on neo-liberal (i.e. free-market) values, some people (and countries) will be prone to exploitation because their **endowments** (resources, labour and capabilities) will only earn them a subsistence **entitlement**.

The poor therefore need to be protected from the worst excesses of the market and helped to develop their capabilities and resources.

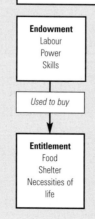

Endowment
Labour
Power
Skills

Used to buy

Entitlement
Food
Shelter
Necessities of life

Each of us has an **endowment** which we can use to gain the commodities we need in order to survive. Our endowment includes the resources we own, our labour and other capabilities which can be exchanged for food and other necessities.

Our **entitlement** is the bundle of commodities we can obtain legitimately in exchange for our endowment. If our entitlement is not large enough, our survival may be threatened and, in the worst case, we may starve.

7.4 THE 'NEW ECONOMY'

Key Ideas 🔑

The 'New Economy'

In the USA, economists and business analysts have coined the term '**New Economy**' to describe the conditions underlying the American 'economic miracle' of the 1990s.

Advocates of the New Economy believe that it may be possible for a smoothly working economy based on competition, globalisation and ultra-rapid communications to yield much higher rates of economic growth than in the past.

However, the events of September 11th also reveal that shocks to the economic system can suddenly slow down the entire process of economic growth, leading to the kind of widescale recessions more often associated with the 'old economy'.

Growth in internet-based businesses (**dot.coms**) and high-tech industries helped to raise living standards in the USA throughout the 1990s.

But the terrorist attack on the World Trade Center in New York in September 2001 had an immediate impact, not just on the American economy, but on business confidence throughout the world, plunging many economies into recession.

Moreover, while the benefits of the New Economy may be available to advanced-technology nations like the USA, many parts of the world still operate a 'pre-internet' economy.

Doctor Proctor outlines... WHAT'S NEW ABOUT THE NEW ECONOMY?

The New Economy has two important characteristics:

1 It appears to be able to sustain a much lower level of unemployment than in the past without leading to a rise in the rate of inflation (which has decreased from 6% in the late 1970s to about 4% today). This is partly the result of increasing competition in both national and international markets, not least in the labour market.

2 It is highly productive. The underlying growth rate of productivity in the US economy rose sharply in the 1990s, largely as a result of globalisation and information technology.

An interesting aspect of the leap forward in GDP in the USA was the fact that national income rose much faster than output. Statisticians could easily calculate the incomes people took away in their pockets. However, rises in productivity were much more difficult to measure because there were so many new products hitting the market.

As with any revolution, it took time for industry to reorganise itself around the innovations.

7.5 THE EURO

The European Single Currency

The Euro – from January 2002, the official currency of the European Union

From January 2002 the **Euro** became the official currency of the European Union. Euro notes and coins became the common means of exchange and banking within all countries signed up to the single currency. Initially 11 countries signed up, but other European Union countries are expected to follow.

In order to move towards a common currency, the economies of these countries have to **converge**, e.g. to reduce their government budget deficits to an agreed low percentage. They must also achieve a common low inflation and interest rate figure. During this time, their currencies are able to move up and down (within set limits) against the Euro.

A **European Central Bank** has been set up to administer the interest rate policy of the Eurozone.

Doctor Proctor outlines... THE EURO: FOR AND AGAINST

The Euro: Arguments For

Many large businesses are in favour of the Euro because:

1 They no longer have to incur the **transaction costs** of currency conversion – for example, changing francs into lire.

2 Businesses in countries signed up to the single currency no longer have to worry about fluctuations in exchange rates. For example, in the past, a French business that sold goods on credit to Germany might have lost out if the franc lost value against the mark before payment became due.

Within the European Union today, each country conducts over half its trade with its EU partners. Having a single currency reduces transaction costs within this single market.

The Euro: Arguments Against

The main objections to the Euro are:

1 **Economic**. Some EU members are reluctant to hand over more powers to the European Central Bank. The ECB sets interest rates, taking into account the health of the EU as a whole rather than the needs of individual member states.

2 **Nationalistic**. Some see membership of the Euro as a further erosion of Britain's sovereignty. This is symbolised by the replacement of national notes with Euro notes.

Institutional Economics

1 How can ideas and patterns of behaviour become institutionalised over time?
2 How might institutions in some countries make it difficult to implement free-market economic ideas?
3 In what way do institutions raise the transaction costs of economic activity?

Environmental Economics

1 How might economists place values on the environment?
2 Why might a 'willing to pay' test not place an accurate value on an environmental asset?
3 What alternative approach could be used to place a value on an environmental asset?

International Economics

1 What is the difference between **internationalisation** and **globalisation**?
2 What is the difference between **fair trade** and **free trade**?
3 How might the **entitlements** of some people in developing countries be less than they need for survival? What can be done to improve the **endowments** of people in both developing and developed countries?
4 Which of the following factors are likely to have slowed down the move towards freer markets in Russia over the last few years?

   a) The power and influence of the Russian Mafia
   b) Laws preventing people from owning land
   c) Lack of knowledge about the nature of markets
   d) Lack of teaching about entrepreneurial activities in schools
   e) The retention of many powerful positions in society by former high and middle-ranking officials in the Communist Party
   f) Lack of familiarity with the notion of free enterprise
   g) Limited experience of running a stock exchange.

5 Which of the following have encouraged the move to a global economy?

   a) The work of the WTO in progressively reducing tariff barriers
   b) The growth of multinational companies
   c) Trade wars between the USA and Europe
   d) The development of free trade
   e) The growth of the Euro and the dollar as international currencies
   f) The failure of some countries to repay their debts
   g) Rapid improvements in communications and telecommunications.

The 'New Economy'

1 What evidence is there to justify the term 'New Economy'?
2 Does the New Economy guarantee ongoing improvements in living standards?

The Euro

1 List four countries currently using the Euro.
2 Why is economic convergence essential for countries wishing to establish a common currency?
3 How might British businesses benefit from being part of the Eurozone?
4 A survey revealed that the introduction of Euro notes and coins in January 2002 led to a sharp drop in public opposition to Britain joining the single currency. The balance of opinion against entry among voters dropped to 18%, the lowest level since January 1999, according to a quarterly poll of more than 20,000 voters carried out by MORI.

What particularly impressed people surveyed was the successful management of the transition to the Euro and the increasing number of pro-Euro reports in the press.

Why do you think people in this country may be more in favour of joining the Euro than in the past? Give one reason why a Briton who enjoys travelling in Europe might be in favour of Britain joining the single European currency.

The data in this question is designed to draw together some of your learning from Unit 7.

The Institutional Economics of Douglas C. North

Nobel laureate Douglas C. North is one of the world's most influential exponents of institutional economics.

North defines institutions as 'any socially imposed constraint upon human behaviour'. Institutions embody the 'rules of the game' for human interaction. They exist within a society and develop over time. For example, it is an 'institution' in our society that I do not get out of my car and punch the motorist in the next vehicle because I do not like the music he or she is playing on his or her radio.

North states that this sort of institution is enforced at three levels.

- **First-party** enforcement means there is self-enforcement: I abide by the standards set in society because I would be ashamed to give offence.
- **Second-party** enforcement is by retaliation. I do not attack the other motorist because they might hit me back.
- **Third-party** enforcement is wider and includes the threat of public loss of face, and more importantly in this case, enforcement by the police and the law courts.

North shows that in market terms, the larger the economy, the greater the need for governmental and intergovernmental enforcement. Hence the role of institutions like the World Trade Organisation, the World Bank and the International Monetary Fund.

In order for a market to work effectively, a country needs social institutions which support the market framework – for example, the first-, second- and third-party mechanisms that ensure that contracts are honoured. These institutions must work smoothly to avoid creating unnecessary transaction costs which raise prices and make businesses and countries uncompetitive. In order for a country to work on free-market lines, it needs to have institutions which support this structure – e.g. property rights, contractual rights, a culture of enterprise and hard work, expectations that debtors will pay on time, etc.

In North's view, one of the major reasons we do not have a truly global economy is that this would require a global government. There would have to be enforcement mechanisms that could be applied internationally.

Doctor Proctor's DATA QUESTIONS

1 Give an example of an institution associated with a free-market society and show how this is enforced at each of the three levels outlined by North.	2 Why might it be difficult to impose free-market solutions on an economy which lacks the institutions to support such a structure?
	3 Why is a world government a necessary condition for a truly global economy?

Answers

Unit 1: Introduction

The Importance of Economics

i) Education: (a)
ii) New technology: (b)
iii) Income tax: (c)
iv) Concentrating on best lines: (a)
v) Concentrating on disabled: (a) and (c)

Economic Incentives

i) A tax or fine on pollution creation. Grants to create or improve pollution removal processes
ii) Bonuses for meeting set targets, coupled with non-money rewards such as subsidised goods for meeting performance targets
iii) Tax breaks or reductions for money and time contributed to the community
iv) Subsidies and grants to support organic farming.

Opportunity Cost

Buying a new shirt is the opportunity cost, because this is the next-best alternative that is sacrificed.

The Macro and Micro Economy

i) Unemployment levels in the UK: macro
ii) Unemployment levels in Rochdale: micro
iii) Inflation in Europe: macro
iv) The price of cheese in a local market: micro
v) The exchange rate of the Euro against the dollar: macro
vi) The rise of living standards in a country: macro

Supply and Demand

Demand:

i) Demand curve shifts to the right as consumers switch from the rival paper.
ii) Demand shifts to right as tastes change in favour of newspaper reading.
iii) Demand shifts to left because fall in income levels leaves people with less disposable income.
iv) Demand shifts to the left as some customers switch to the rival paper.
v) Movement takes place up the demand curve, as the price of the paper increases – consumers buy less at the same price than they did before.
vi) Demand shifts to left as fewer commuters buy papers.

Supply:

i) Supply shifts to the left because of increased cost of production.
ii) Supply shifts to the right as new technology enables cost reductions.
iii) Supply shifts to the left as labour costs increase.

The Price System

i) The equilibrium price is 30 pence because at this price both demand and supply are for 160 million packets. The desires of both suppliers and demanders are met.
ii) At 10 pence demand would far exceed supply – by 320 million packets. At 10 pence, suppliers would not be prepared to supply to the market. At 40 pence, demand would only be for 80 million packets while supply would be for 240 million packets, leaving 160 million packets unsold – forcing a reduction in price towards the equilibrium.

Unit 2: Economic Goals

Economic Growth

1 National Income can be calculated by adding together factor incomes (**income method**), final expenditures (**expenditure method**) and the value added by individual industries (**output method**).

2 To move from GDP at factor cost to national income, you must first add the net inflow of **property income** from abroad. You must then deduct any **depreciation** in machinery and plant.

3 To move from domestic demand figures to GDP you need to include the international trade sector. Domestic demand may be higher than GDP if exports are higher than imports.

4 The impact 'cowboys' make on the world they live in is negligible because of the healing forces of nature. In contrast, people travelling in a 'spaceship' live in an enclosed environment in which resources are severely limited. The reality is that we live in a spaceship: we should not think and act as if we were cowboys.

Inflation

1 The RPI shows the average change in the price of a basket of goods bought by a 'typical' household in the UK, based on survey data. A base year is used to calculate price changes. RPIX, or the underlying rate, takes out the impact of changes in mortgage interest rates.

2 Businesses prefer inflation to be at a steady and low rate, because this provides the stability to enable smooth and easily calculable transactions. In a time of low inflation, businesses will be pleased to supply goods on credit, and a low inflation rate will support the international competitiveness of industry.

3   In a period of inflation, **pensioners**, **savers**, and others on **fixed incomes** can lose out. Beneficiaries will include **borrowers** and those who hold **property** and other appreciating assets.

4   Imported inflation occurs when the price of imports, e.g. oil, is rising – thus adding to production costs in this country. This is a form of cost-push inflation.

Unemployment

1   The trade cycle causes cyclical unemployment during economic downswings because there is a general fall in the level of demand in the economy. **Seasonal unemployment** – falling demand for labour at certain times of the year – is another form of demand inflation. **Structural unemployment** results from a changing structure in demand in the economy, leading to the growth of some industries and the decline of others.

2   The supply side can be improved by reducing frictions in the marketplace. For example, by:

- exposing industry to higher levels of **competition**
- **reducing barriers** to entry, e.g. trade union restrictions on the flexibility of labour
- **reducing tax rates** which discourage investment and enterprise.

3   i)   Wasted resources
     ii) Higher taxes to support the unemployed
     iii) Lack of training for those out of work (no on-the-job training).

4   The graph below shows the effect of introducing a minimum wage of £5.

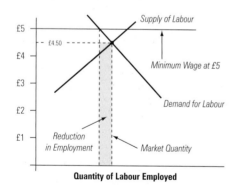

Quantity of Labour Employed

The Balance of Payments

1   Visible exports: whisky, Jaguar cars, Cadbury's Flake.
     Visible imports: Honda cars, washing machines, American computers.

2   **Visibles** are tangible goods that can be touched and seen. **Invisibles** are services such as banking, insurance and transport services.

3   The **current account** shows trading in goods and services. The **capital account** shows international borrowing and lending. The **balance for official financing** shows the increase or decrease in foreign currency reserves.

4   The exchange rate is the rate at which the currency of one country, e.g. the Euro in the European Union, is exchanged for another currency, e.g. the US dollar.

Other Economic Goals

1   'Equity' is a value-laden concept. Some people believe that we should all have equal shares of the cake, others believe that those who work harder should receive bigger slices.

2   Intergenerational equity is concerned with handing on to the next generation at least *as much* as we have inherited ourselves. It is best achieved through sustainable development.

3   Intragenerational equity is concerned with fair distribution among people sharing the planet at the same time. This is best achieved by fair trade and concern for the development needs of those areas which are less well endowed with resources, particularly investment capital.

4   'Sustainable development' is a value-laden concept. It involves intergenerational and intragenerational equity, as well as a long-term concern for nature and the environment.

5   Hard-line environmentalists maintain that it is not possible to make 'trade-offs' with nature. Those with less rigid views believe that it is possible to exchange a little less nature for a little more man-made capital. David Pearce argues that if trade-offs are to be made, we need to place a value on nature so that we know the value of what we are sacrificing.

Data Question

1   The goods sector of the economy is experiencing deflation, i.e. the sector producing physical products such as cars, electronic goods, food, etc. Deflation means a general fall in the level of prices so that there are negative changes.

2   Services – e.g. hairdressing, door-to-door post delivery, personal banking – are more labour-intensive than goods. Many of the operations involved are of a personal nature – e.g. treatment in a hospital. This means that it is more difficult to introduce automation.

3   Over time as people become more wealthy they can afford to buy more services. As demand increases relative to supply, the demand curve shifts to the right, pushing up prices.

4   As supply increases over time in the goods sector, particularly as a result of falls in the cost of production, the supply curve shifts to the right, leading to a fall in prices.

5 France, Germany, Japan.

6 In the early 2000s, demand was rising, but not as quickly as supply. For example, the events of September 11th led to a reduction in demand for air travel and tourism. At the same time, the supply of goods continued to increase following improvements in technology, and distribution. The net effect was that supply was more buoyant than demand, leading to falling prices. In addition, many governments were more effective in controlling inflation than they were previously.

7 Inflation can be revived by shocks to the world supply system such as wars, and also by increasing levels of demand.

Unit 3: Achieving Economic Goals

Economic Tools

Interest Rate

If the supply of money increases this is likely to force down interest rates.

Taxation

i) Taxes on wines and spirits: indirect
    Income tax: direct
    VAT: indirect
    Corporation tax: direct
    National Insurance: direct
    Taxes on cigarettes: indirect
    Council tax: direct
ii) Corporation tax

Government Spending

i) Social services, NHS, Education
ii) Capital spending

Regional Policy

Examples include tax relief and grants on investment, employment subsidies, provision of ready-built factory buildings and offices.

Exchange Rate

When the Eurozone runs a balance of payments surplus, Euros are in greater demand than supply. This pushes up the price of the Euro.

Applying Economic Tools

Fiscal Policy

Automatic stabilisers take money out of the system when it is booming and put money back in during a recession, e.g. unemployment benefits rise and fall with employment levels.

Monetary Policy

i)   Interest rates
ii) Money supply
iii) Control of credit.

In a downturn, interest rates could be lowered, money supply increased and credit controls relaxed.

Exchange Rate Policy

If the pound is too low this can lead to imported inflation, and import prices become relatively more expensive. This is a form of **cost-push inflation**.

Economic Theory

Classical Economics

In a free market, consumers vote with their money, spending for what they want to produce. Suppliers respond in order to make a profit. The market is the mechanism which enables allocative efficiency.

Keynesian Economics

The government can increase its own spending (and/or lower taxes), hence stimulating wider increases in aggregate demand in the economy.

The 'New Economy'

The New Economy is characterised by low inflation and low unemployment. This is the result of higher levels of competition, increasing use of new technology, and the removal of restrictions within the economy.

Comparing Economic Theories

i) a; ii) c; iii) b; iv) a; v) b; vi) c; vii) a; viii) b; ix) c; x) b; xi) a.

Data Question

1 The Monetary Policy Committee is made up of independent experts, mainly economists and financial specialists, whose job is to set an interest rate each month that will enable the government to achieve its target inflation rate of 2.5%. The MPC was set up by the current chancellor of the exchequer, Gordon Brown, to provide independent control over a major aspect of economic policy. Previously, responsibility for determining the interest rate lay with the chancellor, who had often manipulated it for political rather than economic ends, leading to an increase in inflation.

2 Reducing interest rates cuts the cost of borrowing and repaying loans. This makes it easier for businesses to supply larger quantities of products, to make more profits and to be more competitive.

3 The case for a cut in interest rates is that parts of the economy such as manufacturing are experiencing deflationary conditions. Manufacturers are laying off workers because of rising costs and falling orders accentuated by the high exchange rate.

4 The problem with cutting the interest rate is that this may encourage too much borrowing, which may lead to an increase in inflation. Also, some borrowers may not be able to repay their debts.

Unit 4: Government and the Private Sector

Public and Private

  i) Window-cleaning business: private
 ii) The BBC: public
iii) A cleaning business: private
 iv) Virgin Trains: private
  v) A municipal enterprise: public
 vi) A public company: private
vii) A public corporation: public

The Case for Private Ownership

  i) Adam Smith believed that by pursuing their own self-interest, individuals create the greatest wealth and well-being for all. Resources are channelled into those forms of activity which best meet individual needs and hence the needs of society. Producers respond to the wishes of consumers.

 ii) Competition is seen as the spur to efficiency and to the best possible use of resources. In a market economy, businesses compete to use resources in the most efficient way.

The Case for State Control

  i) It may not be feasible on cost grounds for private enterprises to supply goods and services to small numbers of people in remote areas. With state provision, one group of consumers can subsidise another, e.g. people in cities can pay higher postal charges to support services to people in rural areas.

 ii) State control of Railtrack could ensure that long-term rather than short-term considerations are taken into account, particularly in terms of major investment projects. The state is also more likely to put social considerations such as safety above profit.

Why Privatise?

- British Telecom, the steel industry, the coal industry, the electricity companies and British Rail were all privatised in the period 1979–97.
- The owners of the privatised industries are the **shareholders**.
- The public is protected against the poor running of the privatised companies by independent **regulators** and **consumer committee**s. Privatised companies are also monitored by a government minister, and questions can be asked in Parliament.

Maximising Efficiency

- **Allocative efficiency** occurs when resources are used in line with consumer requirements. **Productive efficiency** involves using resources in the most efficient way, minimising cost and waste.

- The BBC has been seeking to achieve greater productive efficiency by breaking the organisation down into profit centres. Each profit centre must make a market return on money invested in it. Cross-subsidisation (where a profit-making unit channels some of its profits to a non-profit-making unit) has been eliminated by creating an internal market structure. Resources therefore have to be used in an efficient way.

- The BBC seeks to achieve allocative efficiency by researching into what consumers want and delivering the kind of programmes that meet their needs. However, the BBC must do more than simply provide low-brow mass entertainment.

- Privatising the BBC would force it to focus on meeting private-sector efficiency criteria. This would help cut out further production inefficiencies and ensure a more sharply focused operation. However, if the BBC were privatised, it would no longer serve the needs of the nation – it would focus on creating shareholder value. As a result, it might lose its international reputation for impartiality and become just another mass-market broadcaster.

The Third Way

- The Third Way seeks to combine a neo-liberal market philosophy with social values. It is based on the notion of **inclusivity**, i.e. building a broad community in which no groupings are excluded. It involves applying private-sector funds and ways of working to forms of social provision such as education and health.

- The Third Way departs from the traditional neo-liberal view of allocative efficiency. However, it may give rise to new forms of allocative efficiency based on meeting the wider needs of society. The danger of the Third Way is that it may lead to productive inefficiency (as in the case of the minimum wage, which prevents market clearing). If market criteria can be applied to the public sector, it may be possible to improve productive efficiency in this sector. However, critics question whether private-sector criteria are appropriate in social welfare provision.

- The Third Way is associated with:

  i) encouraging private/public partnerships
iii) allowing competition in postal delivery services
  v) supporting the principle of a mixed economy
 vi) handing over control for setting interest rates to the MPC
vii) encouraging social inclusion
viii) developing social investment schemes.

Data Question

1 Privatisation is the process of selling a formerly state-run organisation to the private sector. Private-sector concerns like Railtrack are owned by shareholders.

2 The dangers of privatising Railtrack were that a number of social criteria might be sacrificed to private gain. For example, running the service on time might take priority over safety. Providing train services to remote areas might be sacrificed to concentrating on the most profitable lines.

3 The failure of Railtrack highlights the problem of combining profit with public service. In the private sector there is a major emphasis on value for shareholders. This can mean that wider social considerations are neglected. Large-scale public concerns such as the NHS, education and transport cannot be run using the same criteria as a supermarket or coca-cola plant.

4 A not-for-profit company is one in which profit is secondary to wider social objectives. In the case of the rail network, this approach would allow priority to be given to other objectives such as safety and public service.

Unit 5: Rewards to Factors of Production

Factors of Production

- Oil reserves: land
- Oyster beds: land
- Skilled car fitters: labour
- Shareholders: enterprise
- A business owner: enterprise
- Machinery: capital
- An oil rig: capital
- A roadsweeper: labour
- A machine tool: capital
- A teacher: labour
- A franchise: enterprise

Rewards to Factors of Production

a) £30,000 (Yield from Potatoes minus Yield from Turnips)

b) £70,000 (what the land could earn in its next-best use, i.e. turnip production)

Wage Levels in the Market

1 Doctors are in shorter supply than nurses because of the higher level of entry qualification and the greater length of training required. However, nurses are also scarce relative to the demand for them – which is why many nurses have to be recruited from overseas. There may also be an element of sex discrimination involved, in that a doctor is traditionally a male occupation. It is possible also that nurses are exploited because many feel that they have a 'vocation' and have traditionally been reluctant to take industrial

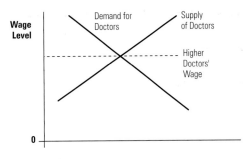

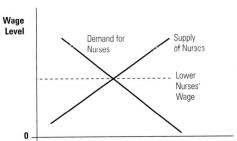

action. The intensity of demand for doctors is also higher than that for nurses.

2 An increase in the supply of foreign nurses is likely to reduce nurses' wages in the long run.

3 A minimum wage set at 0W is above the market-clearing wage rate. As a result, some cleaners will lose their jobs or be forced to work 'on the black' (i.e. take part in the 'black' or unofficial economy) at levels below the minimum wage.

The Demand for and Supply of Capital

If the interest rate falls to 5%, a greater number of investment opportunities will be taken up because there will be more opportunities where the marginal efficiency of capital is higher than the interest rate.

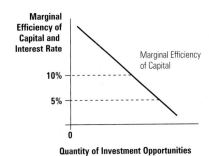

Quantity of Investment Opportunities

Enterprise and Profit

New firms are enticed into the industry by the possibility of making abnormal profits. As a result competition intensifies, reducing the profitability of the firm that originally enjoyed the monopoly.

If competition continues to intensify, it is possible that the original monopolist may find itself in a position where its profits fall below the normal profit level. At this point, there is a strong incentive for it to leave the industry.

Who Benefits?

Equity and **equality** can mean the same thing if you believe that a fair situation is one based on equality. However, if your view of fairness includes the notion that a degree of inequality might act as a spur to enterprise, the two concepts will differ.

Equity is thus based on subjective definitions of fairness, just as equality is based on different forms of equality – equality of opportunity, equality of access, equality of outcomes, etc.

Data Question

1 Some workers are earning as much as £722 per week. Their wages will be higher than the wage they could earn in their next-best alternative occupation. This surplus over and above opportunity cost is termed **economic rent**. Even workers on much lower wages are in a position to earn economic rent.

2 People at the bottom of the pile may not be able to gain any alternative work. Therefore just like the least fertile land they accrue no surplus – and therefore no economic rent.

3 Reasons why financial workers in the City earn more include:
   i) They are willing to work unsocial hours.
   ii) There is high demand for their skills, and relatively scarce supply.
   iv) Costs of living and working in the City are high.
   v) Financial workers make a high contribution to productivity.
   vi) Non-economic factors such as favouritism and patronage (the 'old boy network') may enable them to earn artificially high wages.

4 Explanations for the difference between men's and women's wages include:
   i) Differences in nature of work done and supply/demand relationships in these jobs
   ii) Differences in ability and availability to work unsocial hours
   iii) Differences in levels of education and training
   iv) Prejudice and discrimination.

Unit 6: Economics of the Firm

Costs and Revenues

1 Cost for the chocolate factory are divided as follows:
   • Wages which are linked directly to output: *variable*
   • Management salaries: *fixed*
   • Rent and rates on premises: *fixed*
   • Raw material costs: *variable*
   • Lighting costs in the factory: *fixed*

   • Water used directly in the production process: *variable*

2 The contribution per book is £5, the difference between the buying and selling price. If fixed costs are £1,000, it would therefore take the contribution of 200 books to pay off the fixed costs. Break-even is therefore 200 books.

Economies of Scale

Economies of scale are simply the advantages of producing many products rather than a few. They can be technical, managerial, labour, marketing, financial, etc.

A hotel chain would be able to employ specialist managers, enabling more efficient management of accounts and customer relations. A large hotel could also benefit from technical advantages of scale, by being able to deal with a much larger number of guests through a central reception desk.

Internal economies are:
   i)   investment in new technology
   iii) the preferential loan arrangement
   iv) global advertising
   viii) discounts on training

The others are external economies.

The 'Perfect Market'

   • An **identical product** means that consumers do not have to spend time making comparisons: they know what they are getting for their money.
   • **Ease of entry** means that new firms can enter the market if competition is reduced in any way, or if abnormal short-term profits are to be made
   • **Perfect information** means that consumers can make choices based on a full knowledge of what is available, rather than having to guess.

Monopoly

Allocative efficiency does not occur under a monopoly because the monopolist is able to restrict output, thus withholding products from consumers. Those that the monopolist sells are sold at more than their marginal cost of production.

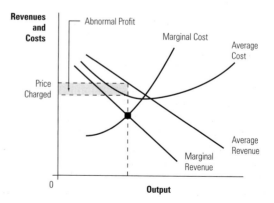

Competition among the Few

Examples include high street banking, book publishing, confectionery manufacture, car production, top divisions for country cricket and football.

In a sector such as banking, competition is intense for company accounts. Points of comparison between banks can include: service offered, simplicity of accounts, integration between accounts, return on savings and penalties on negative balances.

The following are characteristic of a competitive oligopoly:

iii) New firms are able to enter the market.

iv) There are relatively few firms in the market.

v) Products are differentiated.

vi) Rival firms compete aggressively.

vii) Firms are generally aware of what rivals are doing.

viii) Firms compete through advertising.

ix) Firms compete to become the market leader.

Data Question

1 The chief barrier to entry is the sheer scale of any internet book-distributing business, requiring the holding of large numbers of titles and the negotiation of preferential discounts with many different book suppliers. Another barrier is the strong position of booksellers in the parallel, high street book market.

2 Competition is determined by ease of entry into the market, the number of sellers, the similarity of internet sites, the extent to which potential customers are prepared to spend time searching the net to compare prices, lists, etc.

3 Factors restricting Amazon from making monopoly profits are the existence of rival internet booksellers, particularly established firms with a web-based offshoots, the high costs of distributing books, the relative ease of entry into internet commerce, and the ease with which consumers can buy books through conventional bookshops.

4 First mover advantage is the advantage of being first on the market and then continually keeping ahead of the field by developing new advantages based on experience in the industry.

5 The difficulty of sustaining this advantage is that, in some ways, Amazon is starting behind its traditional rivals, who have many years of competing in this industry. Although Amazon may be able to build up some key advantages over rivals in the early days, these will diminish as time goes on, enabling rivals to catch up. The key is to gain the lion's share of the market and then to benefit from scale economies.

Unit 7: New Ideas in Economics

Institutional Economics

1 Over time, patterns of behaviour become the established norms of society and are cemented into place by social convention and repeated practice. People are born into an institutionalised society and they adopt its conventions and patterns of behaviour as being 'normal'.

2 A country may not have the financial and business institutions required, e.g. a capital market, Stock Exchange, etc. Its people may have no idea how these institutions function, and will need time to develop habits of saving and profit-making. The transition to a free-market economy cannot be achieved by a 'Big Bang' or 'quick fix' solution.

3 Institutions raise transactions costs because every hurdle in the way of a smooth-running system has a cost in time or money. For example, the cost of a long-drawn out legal procedure may make a marginal project unjustifiable.

Environmental Economics

1 Through a process of monetisation and questionnaire, people can be asked to place values on the environment or parts of it – e.g. through 'willing to pay' questions.

2 With 'willing to pay' approaches, people are asked to assign values using imaginary sums of money which they know they will never have to spend, and which are no more than 'figures plucked from the air'. Research into this approach shows that people will often give different values when presented with the same question.

3 An alternative question is: 'How much would you want to receive *in compensation for the loss of* an environmental asset?' This usually leads to a higher valuation being placed on the asset in question.

International Economics

1 **Internationalisation** involves the extension of international trade over time and is about quantitative change. **Globalisation** involves a qualitative shift to a more integrated world system characterised by freer flows of capital and trade and by the development of independent transnational corporations.

2 **Free trade** involves the elimination of barriers to trade, enabling free buying and selling. **Fair trade** involves making sure that there is no exploitation resulting from relative strength in bargaining position. Often it involves paying an extra cost to assist development in the target country.

3 **Entitlements** imply access to an available resource base from which it is possible to earn a living. Unfortunately entitlements can be depleted

by natural and man-made causes. **Endowments** can be improved by developing inclusive social structures which allow everyone in a community to benefit from exchange and interdependence. This might involve fair trade, or it could involve some form of grassroots development.

4   All of the factors listed are likely to have slowed down the move towards free markets in Russia.

5   Factors encouraging the growth of the global economy have been:

a) The work of the WTO in progressively reducing tariff barriers
b) The growth of multinational companies
d) The development of free trade
e) The growth of the Euro and the dollar as international currencies
f) Rapid improvements in communications and telecommunications.

The 'New Economy'

1   Some argue that the continued period of growth in the US over the last decade of the twentieth century is evidence of the development of a New Economy. Further evidence is the low level of unemployment and inflation during this period, and the impact of new technology. However, the events of September 11th make it difficult to tell to what extent this is a longer-term trend.

2   The New Economy does not guarantee ongoing growth patterns although it provides the potential to reduce costs and to create greater international integration. The adoption of new technologies makes the economy more productive, but does not necessarily involve a move away from the traditional trade cycle.

The Euro

1   Countries currently signed up to the Euro include France, Germany, Italy, the Netherlands, Belgium, Luxembourg and Ireland.

2   Economic convergence ensures that countries have the economic strength to survive within a regime in which economic policies, e.g. monetary policy, are determined centrally. Convergence also helps to create confidence in the Eurozone. For example, if one country had a very high budget deficit, this would undermine confidence in the system.

3   There would be no transaction costs of changing money within the Eurozone. Access to European Union markets would be eased, enabling greater integration between the parts of British businesses operating within this zone.

4   The smooth transition to the Euro and the lack of major problems may have swayed the British public after all the previous anti-Euro publicity. Once a currency is a physical reality, people are far more likely to believe in it.

A British tourist to Europe would be pleased not to have to pay the transaction costs of switching money from one currency to another.

Data Question

1   An example of a free-market institution is the practice of buying and selling goods on credit. At the first level, this is enforced by our own feelings that have been bred into us that we must pay our debts on time. At the second level, the person we owe money to will start making demands on us. At a third level, we may be taken to court and forced to pay the debt.

2   In societies unused to the free market, alternative institutions may already be in place. For example individuals may be used to co-operation rather than competition. Existing social norms and legal structures may discourage competition. In other societies there may be institutionalised systems of bribery and corruption which add to transaction costs.

3   In a global society, the expectation would be that everybody plays by the same set of rules. In a non-global world there are many different governments and many different sets of rules. Often rules and institutions clash. The only way of solving this problem is by creating intergovernmental structures and – ultimately – a world government.

Glossary

Allocative efficiency The efficiency of an economic system in meeting the needs of participants, particularly in giving consumers what they want without exploiting them.

Base year Point of comparison in calculating an index. Figures for subsequent years can be compared with the base figure, which is given a value of 100.

Capital goods Goods that are themselves used in the production of other goods.

Classical economics Economic theory based on the work of Adam Smith and David Ricardo, which explains the creation of wealth and advocates free trade.

Comparative advantage Benefit of concentrating on goods or services in which an individual, organisation or country is 'most best' or 'least worst'.

Conditions of demand or supply Factors other than price which affect demand and supply.

Diminishing returns Progressively smaller increases in output resulting from equal increases in productive factors.

Distribution Division of the total income of a community among its members.

Economic rent Surplus earned by a factor of production over and above its supply price (also referred to as **transfer earning** and **opportunity cost**).

Elastic demand When a change in price leads to a more than proportionate change in quantity demanded.

Goals Aim or objective to which an endeavour is directed, e.g. the goals of government economic policy include low inflation and low unemployment.

Inelastic demand When a change in price leads to a less than proportionate change in quantity demanded.

Institution Established custom, law, or relationship in a society or community.

Keynesian economics Branch of economic theory developed by John Maynard Keynes, in which the government is seen as having a role in managing demand in the economy to compensate for failures in the free market – for example, by raising levels of employment.

Marginal efficiency of capital Anticipated returns from extra units of investment or from each additional investment project.

Monetisation Assigning a monetary value to an asset.

Price elasticity of demand Responsiveness of demand to changes in price.

Price elasticity of supply Responsiveness of supply to changes in price.

Profit motive Incentive effect of profit as a stimulus to business and economic activity.

Free market Unfettered operation of the forces of supply and demand, without control or interference by government.

Inflation Rate of increase of prices.

Opportunity cost Cost of the next-best alternative that is sacrificed when an economic decision is made.

Productive efficiency Producing goods without wasting resources in the production process.

Socialism Economic system in which the means of production, distribution and exchange are owned collectively by the community.

Unitary elasticity When a change in price leads to an identical (but opposite) change in quantity demanded.

World Trade Organisation (WTO) International (now permanent) body tasked with reducing barriers to trade across the globe and acting as intermediary in international trade disputes.

Index